D0114324

THEN & NOW

THEN & NOW

The Personal Past in the Poetry of

Robert Penn Warren

FLOYD C. WATKINS

THE UNIVERSITY PRESS OF KENTUCKY

Scholarly publisher for the Commonwealth,
serving Berea College, Centre College of Kentucky,
Eastern Kentucky University, The Filson Club,
Georgetown College, Kentucky Historical Society,
Kentucky State University, Morehead State University,
Murray State University, Northern Kentucky University,
Transylvania University, University of Kentucky,
University of Louisville, and Western Kentucky University.

Editorial and Sales Offices: Lexington, Kentucky 40506-0024

Library of Congress Cataloging in Publication Data

Watkins, Floyd C., 1920–
  Then & now.

  Includes bibliographical references and index.
  1. Warren, Robert Penn, 1905–   . 2. Poets,
American—20th century—Biography. 3. Warren
family. 4. Kentucky in literature. I. Title.
II. Title: Then and now.
PS3545.A748Z94 1982   813'.52 [B]   81-51016
ISBN 0-8131-1456-X

For Anna

Contents

Preface

WHEN I ASKED Robert Penn Warren to approve my writing about his childhood, he replied that he did not "intend to write an autobiography," but that he did plan "to prepare a few memoranda probably to be held for a few years." As for my study of his early years and the poems about them, he thought, "Atmosphere is what you'll get and that is thin gruel."

I began reading and searching, accumulated a great quantity of information, but acquired very little understanding or insight for a few years. I studied the childhood and collected rumors and facts. The memories of Warren and of the people in the town varied widely, and the discrepancies were so great that in many instances I could only record the unreconciled diversities. I read the poems again and over and over, interviewed Warren, went back to the towns of Guthrie and Cerulean, wrote notes and pieces of chapters and read the poems again and then wrote again. When I finished the account of his childhood, I sent my work to Warren, hoping that I had at least something more than thin gruel.

The poems about Guthrie and Cerulean when assembled as a unit contained Warren's created village of the mind and art. No other poet that I know of in the English language (perhaps there are slight resemblances in Wordsworth and Whitman) has created in diverse poems his childhood community or has written a chronicle of more than a hundred years of the lives of his family in a number of poems. I can recall no scholar/critic who has been fortunate in the way that I have with this subject: Warren created the poems for the world and then wrote elaborate suggestions for this book—first one by one on the chapters and finally (in just as much fullness) about the study as a whole. Surely no poet can do more for his reader than this.

Where there be failures, needless to say, they are mine.

Acknowledgments

I KNOW OF no critic with a greater debt to his subject than I have to Robert Penn Warren, who wrote the poetry, letters to me, comments on my chapters, and comments on the final manuscript. Mrs. Warren, who is the distinguished writer Eleanor Clark, has been personally gracious and kind to me.

Citizens of Warren's home town, Guthrie, Kentucky, have given me much time and information, especially Kent Greenfield, Mr. and Mrs. Thomas Warren, Evelyn Hooser, Thomas M. Allensworth, Sr., Everett Frey, Tommie Louise Warren (Mrs. R. D.) Frey (niece of Robert Penn Warren), John M. Owen, and Lester Lannom. Others from Warren's native county, Todd, in Kentucky who have been especially helpful are Dorothy (Mrs. Frank) McElwain, and Mrs. Marion Williams.

Nan Muth (daughter of Kent Greenfield) and her family have been generous with time and papers.

For advice, reading of the manuscript, information, and other kindnesses I am grateful to William Bedford Clark of Texas A & M University, T.D. Young and Walter Sullivan of Vanderbilt University; James M. Cox of Dartmouth College; George Core of the University of the South; Cornelius Cronin, Anna Nardo, and Lewis Simpson of Louisiana State University; John Hiers of Valdosta State College; Robert Andrew and Charlene Ring of Franklin, Tennessee; Eloise Hamill (Mrs. Clarence) Carney, Richard Bourne, and J. R. Claypool of Nashville; Battle Bagley, Sr., County Historian, Fayetteville, Tennessee; and Patricia Wolcott, genealogist, Ft. Mitchell, Kentucky.

I owe substantial debts to the librarians of the American Literature Collection of the Beinecke Rare Book and Manuscript Library at Yale University; Marice A. Wolfe, Vanderbilt University Library; the Tuskegee Archives, Tuskegee Institute.

I have used much information from the oral history projects at the University of Kentucky and at Western Kentucky University. William Marshall and Claire McCann, of the University of Kentucky Library, were of early and basic assistance.

Friends of Warren who have been informative and kind are Mr. and Mrs. Brainard Cheney, Allen Tate, Caroline Gordon, and Cleanth Brooks.

Citizens of Cerulean, Kentucky, the home town of Warren's parents, who assisted me were Hermit Mitchell, Paul Gardner, and Sara Frances Rascoe.

Emory University has been generous in giving me time off for research, and the Emory University Research Committee has given me time and support. I received a summer research award from the National Endowment for the Humanities. Hugh R. Taylor, of Easton, Connecticut, gave me a much-needed ride on a dark and snowy night.

The Emory University Library has provided me with hours of help far beyond the calls of friendship and duty. I am especially indebted to the Reference Department (Marie Morris Nitzschke and Eric Nitzschke) and the Special Collections (Linda Matthews and Diane Windham).

Students, friends, and colleagues at Emory University have endured my talk of my labors and offered many suggestions: Sally Wolff, Rosemary Magee, Oakley Coburn, John Rozier, Harry Rusche, Frank Manley, William B. Dillingham, Trudy Kretchman and her staff.

Finally, my wife, Anna, has enjoyed the project most with me, helped me constantly, suffered with me, and shared my triumphs.

THEN & NOW

A Note on Sources
& Documentation

THIS BOOK is based on a unique combination of materials: interviews (oral with notes or tape recordings and even sometimes memory), Warren's corrections and suggestions on early drafts and a late version of the manuscript, government documents, letters, oral history projects, vital statistics, information on tombstones, and other varieties of usual and unusual aids to a scholar and critic.

These materials seem to call for a system of documentation unusual in literary studies. At the end of the book is a list of references, numbered and classified. Throughout the work unsequential superscript numbers in the text refer to the sources listed at the end. Thus what appears to be a strange first footnote (16) is actually a reference to a document listed at the back of the book.

In quoting the poetry of Robert Penn Warren, I have used the text in *Selected Poems 1923-1975* (New York: Random House) when the passage needed was in that book. Other quotations are drawn from the following volumes, all also published by Random House: *Brother to Dragons: A Tale in Verse and Voices; Promises: Poems 1954-1956; You, Emperors, and Others: Poems 1957-1960; Now and Then: Poems 1976-1978;* and *Being Here: Poetry 1977-1980.*

◆‖◆

Creation
& Criticism

THE EARLY POETRY of Robert Penn Warren is precise in its concrete imagery, grounded on the earth itself in the particularity of the experiences described in the poems, psychologically rooted in fundamental human states of mind. But it is aloof, general in some ways, usually anonymous in its characters. The relationship between the poet and the poem was known only to Warren, and even though he asserted in later years that some of the early poems were deeply rooted in his personal experience, the poem itself does not provide an example or explanation of its origins.

In Warren's full poetic maturity, however, he changed his practices. He became avowedly more personal and much more explicitly autobiographical. He accepted the principle that "literature feeds on life" and "life feeds on it."[16]* He wrote about things and persons he knew, sometimes without disguise and often without significant change in details from reality to the work of the imagination.

At first glance it is strange to comprehend that Warren's work has a solid basis deriving from extraliterary and unscholastic affairs. His poetic art and some of his literary principles seem to belong to a time of the old scholar before the so-called New Critic had ever stepped to the lectern. Warren is

*Superior numbers in this book refer to the reference list, which begins on page 171.

presumed to be a leader of the New Critics, one of the two who carried the principles of this group into the academic world. Only in moments of vehement argument, lured by the intensity of conviction to make an overstatement of their position, did the New Critics deny the connections between literature and life. But their misreaders, some of them with strategic exaggeration, have accused Warren, his collaborator Cleanth Brooks, and other New Critics of severing literature from its life sources.

In the first edition of *Understanding Poetry* in 1938, Brooks and Warren were so dedicated to the importance of poetry as an art, or poetry as poetry first and only, that they made a proclamation that was a red flag to their scholarly antagonists:

If poetry is worth teaching at all it is worth teaching as poetry. The temptation to make a substitute for the poem as the object of study is usually overpowering. The substitutes are various, but the most common ones are:
   1. Paraphrase of logical and narrative content.
   2. Study of biographical and historical materials.
   3. Inspirational and didactic interpretation.[20]

In a revision in 1950, the two anthologists restated their position to those who thought they had "implied a disregard for historical and biographical study." They tried to correct what some had regarded as a mistake. So they "attempted to view the poem in relation to its historical situation and in relation to the body of the poet's work."[21]

In the third edition of *Understanding Poetry* in 1960, Brooks and Warren tried to provide a context that they had assumed all along:

Poems come out of a historical moment, and since they are written in language, the form is tied to a whole cultural context.
   Poems are read by human beings, which means that the reader . . . must be able to recognize the dramatic implications of the form. In earlier editions of this book we assumed, perhaps too confidently, that these provisos were clearly implicit in our thinking. If, in this revision, we spell them out, that can do no harm.[22]

Warren—a novelist and poet and critic who has been superficially regarded as a primary force in the separation of a poem from everything but its own text—is actually an American regionalist, essayist, social critic, historian, biographer, and philosopher; a thinker supremely concerned with the American experience, identity, and character; a scholar who emphasizes biography, social and cultural background, history and literary history; a novelist who makes as much use of fact and history and cultural context as historians themselves do; and a poet who works accurately with minute and particular details based on reality. He is, then, a New Critic and an Old Scholar—contrapuntally and simultaneously. He would argue that in the field of literature the poet, the reader, and the critic must each play many parts.

No poet in America, perhaps, has made a greater effort than Warren to be a learned practitioner of the devices of his art form and at the same time a knowledgeable scholar aware of the conditions of the world that is his subject. As an artist, Warren has often written about an artist-character who creates from the raw materials of life: Jack Burden writes history about both Cass Mastern and Willie Stark; the unnamed narrator (who is not essentially different from Warren) in *World Enough and Time* retells and recreates the life of Jeremiah Beaumont from old diaries, journals, and records; RPW arranges the poetic and dramatic speeches of the personae of *Brother to Dragons;* and so on, though in a slightly different fashion or perhaps on a lesser scale, in a number of works.

Voluminous as Warren has been as a talker and a critic, he has never written extensively about how life and literature are interrelated: "Literature feeds on life and life feeds on it." But if there is no single volume on this topic, there are numbers of short and cryptic observations. In almost offhand remarks Warren has said as much about the origins of literature and its materials as any American writer. In essays, interviews, panels, speeches, textbooks, and conversations, he has discussed the subject over and over. The mind that once ponders the relationship between reality, the processes of creation, and the created product cannot casually cease its pondering. The principles are

numerous, perhaps infinite. Always at first thought they seem
to be obvious, but many of those who agree to the statements
about the relation of literature and life do not follow up the
agreements in their reading and their critical practices. Some do
not know the life; some, the literature. And perhaps no one will
ever solve the mystery of what goes on in the minds of those
who take fact and imaginatively create a work of art related to
it. Warren's theory, constructed from statements that resemble
Heraclitean fragments, is as good and as complete as any I know
—given the premise that the subject can exist only in fragments
and pieces of theories. The principles Warren states about life,
the creative process, and the product are so commonsensical, so
respectful of the mysteries of the imagination, so thoroughly
grounded on a profound understanding of the world and the
possibilities or perhaps the need for a supernatural world, and
so consistently posited that it is usually difficult and unnecessary to expand, contradict, or even explicate his views.

One kind of catalogue of Warren's fiction might be constructed by simply making a list of the incidents, people, situations, and crises of American, especially Southern, history that
he has written about. Among them are Floyd Collins's entrap-
ment in a cave, the life and death of Huey Long, the Sharp-
Beauchamp murder; the list would include the backgrounds of
almost all the books. The fiction from the first was always in
some sense factual and historical. The early poems were more
often general rather than particular, but beginning in the 1950s
most of the poems have identifiable personal and historical
origins somewhat in the fashion of the fiction.

There are resemblances (and sometimes drastic contrasts)
between Warren and the American writers that he has studied
most—Melville, Dreiser, Whittier, Faulkner, Hemingway,
Hawthorne, Emerson, and some others in his anthology of
American literature. Always he attaches much significance to
biography, autobiography, the use by the author of the materials of his life, regional attitudes, family sources, and choices of
subject matter. In his study of Whittier, for example, he sees
relevance in topics like the Whittier family in America, Whittier's reading, the effect of the death of a sister, a legend by

Schoolcraft used as a source, the way "Snow-Bound" "does summarize Whittier's life and work," the obsessive "theme of childhood nostalgia," the timing of a work (it came at "a summarizing moment for the country"), a poem that "is offered as autobiography."[17] As a critic, then, Warren is much concerned with the entire milieu of a work and also with careful and technical critical analysis.

Warren often links several aspects of an author's life with the works he has produced. Thus the old waiter in Hemingway's "A Clean, Well-Lighted Place" "is a brother under the skin to ... Hemingway himself."[19] It follows that to know the work may be to know more about the writer and vice versa. Poems "show the poet's labor of incorporating experience into the life of his consciousness, of setting the past and the present in living dialogue."[115] Experience works through the mind and becomes art. If the poet labors to incorporate, the critic who can find the essential information can also with enlightenment labor to extract elements of the original experience from the poem. Finally, setting the two side by side may result in perception of additional meanings for both.

As a man, a writer, and a critic, Warren looks for the sources of literature and searches for the fact and the past. He has created many characters who are engaged in the same processes. He is as quick to bridle at any denigration of the creative imagination as he is at the suggestion that the source and the work are the same. Although Warren is one of the most learned and well read of the writers of our time, the search for the past, he thinks, is not only intellectual or systematic; he regards it as psychological, emotional, moral, spiritual, even religious. Learning may be imposed upon it or inherent within it, but learning remains incidental. The search for the self and for knowledge is as necessary for an illiterate countryman or a frontiersman as it is for a university philosopher. For all sensitive men, it is an attempt, occasionally successful, to know the self and the relationship of the self to time and place and other people. Origins may be encrusted in filth or glitter, in classical or modern times, American or Southern history. It is a knowledge of the self through an awareness of the evil of community and forebears and through a love of a good self assisted to that goodness through the heroism of another. It survives despite the savage brutalities of criminals and the cruelties of school-boys. The thing sought for is basic and real: it is a gut knowl-edge, so simple that it may be rationally almost incom-prehensible. The search involves the plot, the actions of a seek-ing character. Preparing to write, an author studies his materi-als, takes a trip to the scene of a central event, as Warren went to Smithland, for example, to see the home of Jefferson's neph-ews. In the process of writing, both author and character search for meaning, and through criticism the reader seeks to know the work, then to know it better by studying the writer, hunting out the sources, and then returning for more study of the work itself.

If Warren was ever "unwilling to thrust himself as poet onto centerstage," as Louis D. Rubin believes,[114] in his poetry begin-ning with *Brother to Dragons* in 1953 he became avowedly more personal. He wrote the poem "Mortmain" about going home at the time of the death of his father (1955), and he chose this personal poem for inclusion in an anthology in which contribu-tors were to select their best or most representative poems. Then he wrote "that the poet's personal feelings and convic-tions enter somehow into his poem." Of his own poem, he wrote, "The poem I have chosen here is, clearly, personal. Fur-ther, the personal urgencies are dramatized, are overtly pre-sented, not merely absorbed." He was aware of a change in himself as poet and in his attitude toward the person of the poet in the poetry. "This is the kind of poem I have felt impelled, more and more in late years, though for reasons that are not clear to me, to try."[9] Warren does not even speculate on whether the reasons are personal and nostalgic or esthetic. Whatever they are, they do put the poet in the poem, and one who knows something of the poet and his father and their relationship may speculate on how the literature has fed on life and (in turn) how the reader and life may feed on the liter-ature.

With many writers, the initial conception of a literary work springs from a striking concrete image, an incident, a person—

almost anything that, first, makes a vivid impression on the mind and, second, causes the imagination to leap from that primal cause to a vision of almost an entire work of art. Weeks, months, or years of detailed labor may lie ahead, but the imprint of the striking moment of conception will remain on the final product. Conrad's works often began with this kind of frozen moment; so did Faulkner's (witness the vision of the muddy drawers of the little girl Caddy climbing a tree to look in at a funeral); so did James's (remember the statements of the moments of first creation in the prefaces to nearly all the novels in the New York Edition); so did Warren's.

If Warren's criticism, interviews, and comments are not exactly from the poet's workshop as Eliot said his essays were from his, he always seems to write about other writers with his own life, mind, and experience at least implicitly in mind. (It may be that good critics can never leave their own identities out of their interpretations.) Coleridge has been one of Warren's preoccupations, but the writer who has attracted him most and who is most similar to him is Melville. They mingle the philosophical meaning and the blood of life similarly. "For all Melville's metaphysical passion and thirst for ultimates, his creative mind," Warren wrote about him, "could work only from the stimulation of the concrete, the specific." Further, "Melville had, in a very special way, a mind that could be truly stirred, be fully engaged, only by what was urgently human, and such a subject had to be come upon in life, had to be torn from actual life, with the raw validation of life."[14]

Apparently the moment of conception is not controlled by any conscious self-starter in the poet. Given the writer's entire background, the idea for a work comes from a minute thing but is seen from the perspective of all of the mind. Mystery, then, dominates the creative process from the first "Let there be light." "A poem may, in fact, start from an idea—from a phrase, a scene, an image, or an incident which has, for the poet, a suggestive quality. . . . Or the original item may lead by some more or less obscure train of association to another item which will become the true germ of the poem, and whose symbolic potential may supplant that of the first item." The creative process is "enormously complicated." It occurs "in a flash or it may be laboriously accreted like coral."[12]

"The best parts of a poem," Warren has found, "always come in bursts or in a flash." With "one shot in his gun," the poet hunts for "an unknown beast" and shoots him instantaneously when his aim is right. "You can labor on the pruning" and "you can work at your technique, but you cannot labor the poem into being."[41] Conception is a moment of "contact with reality" and of "shock"; "a lot of current can come through a small wire."[3] Shot or shock or flash, there is surprise, abruptness, recognition, and unquestioning certainty. "It comes"; the poet may not *call* it. "You can't plan the thing itself. It has to come completely fulfilled. Or have the germ of fulfillment."[31] It almost seems as if the mind, the receiver, is completely passive, like a body receiving a bullet in the dark. The control comes from the preparation, the sensitivity, the ability to perceive the shock or shot when it comes. The mind of the creative artist, though passive perhaps for a moment, is a sensitive target unshielded with lead.

Over and over Warren has tried to describe the characteristics of the moment of conception of a literary work; it is almost as if he is telling beginning writers how to know when they are hit by the bullet, or perhaps reminding himself how it feels when the impact of the bullet jolts him. The descriptions of the initial moment of creation can be stated and repeated and revised, but not codified as laws. One may meditate at length on a number of statements Warren has made about the moment of germination:

"When I went back to writing short poems, the poems were more directly tied to a realistic base of facts. . . . They were closer to me, closer to my observed and felt life. They had literal germs. That doesn't mean they were autobiographical in the rigid sense of the word."[33]

"More and more for me the germ of a poem is an event in the natural world. And there is a mood, a feeling that helps."[40]

"Planning is a strange thing. . . . How can you say that you plan a thing that happens in a flash? The word pops into your head."[31] Further: "It only pops into the 'prepared' head, and then raises a million questions. Why did Caedmon suddenly become a poet? Because he slunk away from the harpers from shame?"[95]

"The process is an image of the possibility of meaning growing from experience."[115]

"Almost all, I guess *all,* of the novels I've written and many of the poems get started years before they are written, many years before. . . . Usually there's a long period of thinking the story over, staying with the story or staying with the poem."[38]

These are not laws governing the moments of creation, but descriptions of how it has happened. No one else can take Warren's statements and begin to write poems according to his dicta. Assuming the sensitive and long accumulation of experience, literature begins with chance or accident, startling impression, rapid reaction, and perhaps interpretation. It is a mystery. "But a man has to prepare himself for years," Warren says, "by immersing himself *simultaneously* in life (experience, thought, dream, and labor)." No one can advise another how to make it occur. No one can consciously worry it into existence. But if a person is imaginative, the moment of conception, whatever kind of mystery it is, will happen to him. The only valid advice is to have paper and pencil—if one wishes to preserve the inspiration of that moment—and write it down. Some moments seethe and boil in the imagination without ever becoming a written word for years, and great, truly great, moments of poetic insight occur without ever being written down more often than anyone has ever dreamed of.

The initial moment of conception may come from the remembrance of things past or, as Wordsworth says, from moments of "the spontaneous overflow of powerful feelings" which "originate from emotion recollected in tranquility." Whether from the past or the present, that initial stimulus usually involves the author's recollections of his traditions and his childhood—plus the values and intellectual interpretation, consciously or unconsciously received. Warren knew "the way Negro field hands talked or hill men talked, what they did and what they ate. . . . I was just naturally steeped in it and I knew that world. I also had read a good deal of Southern history and was partly raised by a grandfather who was a great reader of history and talked it all the time."[37] He speaks of having a "fascination with heredity," and observes that adults "continue their boyhood."[32] And further:

"You're stuck with your own experiences, your own world around you."[28]

"All writers are born into a special time, a special place, and a special body of beliefs."[8]

"The basic images that every man has, I suppose, go back to those of his childhood. He has to live on that capital all his life."[30]

A writer born outside any meaningful community (as most Americans are these days) and also born outside any strong family tradition or religion, I believe, will turn to the materials of psychological self-contemplation, or reveries about the erratic or erotic relationships of irrational and chaotic worlds. But a writer born within a tradition and living as a member of a close-knit family group in a small community will return to subjects of childhood in that community or other societies like it. If he writes about a different subject, the geographical and cultural and moral perspective will still be governed most of the time by his native origins. "This would not mean," according to Warren, "that he accepts an inherited world—it means that he must both *see* and criticize its values." A writer who turns to an almost completely foreign culture and community will still see that new world from viewpoints provided him as a child. A black reared in a ghetto or a white Anglo-Saxon Protestant child will see Europe as it would look to person with his particular and individual rearing. Thus Warren may write fiction about Huey Long or a Hungarian Jew, but it will be fiction written by a native of Guthrie, Kentucky. Warren knows that native and provincial restriction (limitation is too strong a word), and he has written in that knowledge all his years. If ever in practice he tried to forget his origins, ironically that time came when he was living among the Fugitives and then the Agrarians or in the years following closely upon those associations. Indeed, Warren's least Southern and most general poetry came before his ten-year furlough from poetry, which began after 1943.

Many critics have discussed Warren's germinal moments of creation, and they have returned to general statements about his use of autobiography in his poetry and fiction. No critic, I believe, has done much more than rephrase what Warren has already said. Indeed, I know of no simpler or better fragments or collections of statements about the preliminary workings of the creative imagination and its materials than those found in Warren's writings. One looks at what he has said and then looks at the work that resulted. One leads to the other. The critic may even see the bright blue arc as the flame jumps, but no psychological, critical, or mental gadget can ever analyze the arc. One states the principles, and one examines the work, and one sees that the principles did indeed follow the work. But he still has not rendered it into its component parts so that he could easily move back and forth between impulse and product. Always the mysteries are left. But the most mysterious of all is how the conception became the art.

The process is still a mystery to Warren himself—even after he has been engaged in it for over a half century. He does not *know* about the ways of literary creation; all he has is a "guess." He conjectures that an artist writes a story when it "has some meaning that you haven't solved in it, that you haven't quite laid hands on." The process is one of search, but also one of tantalizing ignorance. The creator writes to learn, to arrive at an "understanding" of "what its meaning, the potential meaning is." The writer does not begin with understanding: "The story that you understand perfectly, you don't write unless you are a 'professional' writer of fiction. You know what the meaning is; there's nothing there to nag your mind about it. A story that's one for you is the one that you have to work to understand."[44] The mystery of creation is not comfortable. Partly the creator works out of frustration and annoyance, which he hopes will goad him to partial success. Finally, the reader of the created product is also annoyed: he knows that the author did not fully accomplish all that he had hoped, that he never knew exactly what he was doing or how, and that the final work itself (if it is a great work of art) cannot be reduced to a source, a recreation of its origins, a clear and precisely stated meaning, or even a set of clearly related meanings. After all, God said, "Let there be light: and there was light." No one can go behind that, and no one can go far behind the workings of the artist.

If the creating of a work is mysterious, it is also in some ways not of any importance to the critic. The study of the workings of the mind of the creator is not precisely literary study. Warren even maintains that the study of creation per se is of as much interest and value if the resulting work is bad as it is if the product is a masterpiece. The process of creation is of "psychological interest" rather than literary interest.[4] Nor is the identification of sources of primary literary interest. Whether they are drawn from history or less formally recorded "human experience," "their factuality gives them no special privilege." On the other hand, their effects on the work (whether determinable or not) may be of significance. At least, Warren says, "they come [into the mind, I take it] with all the recalcitrances and the weight and the passions of the real world." However factual his sources, the creative artist "must claim to *know* the *inside* of his world for better or for worse. He mostly fails, but he claims to know the inside of his characters, the undocumentable inside." The historian must provide actual documentation; the writer must furnish "the *sense* of this documentation" [italics mine], which may be more difficult than the task of the historian. His "ground rules" are "psychological fact, historical fact, sociological fact, all the various kinds of fact."[29] The actual, then, may seem improbable if the historian has the documentation; the art must be probable, whether the artist has documentation or not. Warren's love of history and his admiration of the historian and his task are among his chief characteristics, but he sees the task of the creative artist as higher than that of the discoverer, recorder, and interpreter. "Stories grow out of place and time, but they also grow, if they are any good, out of the inner struggle of the writer."[2] Even struggle is not enough; it must be struggle to accomplishment.

Somewhere between the germ that starts the growth of the work of art and the finished product is a mysterious world which no one, artist or interpreter, can comprehend. "The primal fecund darkness . . . always lies below our imagination."[11] Creation is "an attenuation, a rehandling, an echo of crude experience."[10] It is like a tunnel of love. The lovers, the artist and his materials, disappear into darkness at one end and emerge into light at the other. If the magic of creation has gone on during the journey, no one should ever tell. Further, even if he wishes to do so, it is impossible for anyone to tell.

The fads of criticism are as variable as the williwaws of the Aleutian Islands. Most criticism at some time between the two major wars of the early twentieth century lost sight of the literary work of art and focused on other and only partially relevant subjects. Then the New Criticism, attempting to set things straight, issued declarations that seemed to isolate the work criticized from everything but the text itself. Such a view was never Warren's. In "A Poem of Pure Imagination" Warren wrote that "all sorts of considerations impinge upon the process" of criticism. Good criticism of a poem, he admitted, is affected by "the spiritual climate of the age," "the over-all pattern of other artistic work by the author in question," "the thought of the author" revealed in "non-artistic sources," "the facts of the author's life." Misunderstandings of the relation between the work and these externals cause "crude historicism, . . . crude psychologism," and other problems.[13]

Criticism that confuses the thing made with the materials from which it is made is "reductive." Warren's colleague Brooks points out that "the biographical and historical facts . . . very frequently prove to be irrelevant to an understanding of that particular work."[1] The study of such irrelevant factors may be a worthwhile intellectual activity, but it is not literary study. The study of the history or geography or any subject related to the poem "tends to move us away from the literary work itself to more general cultural matters." There is nothing wrong with such matters, but there is a great deal wrong with confusing them with literary criticism.

I remember once hearing a pedagogue maintain that students were not profiting from a course because they could not understand what is said, for example, about the rights of women in the *Iliad* and the *Odyssey*. Academically, if the end of knowledge in that classroom was the rights of women, the course should have been given a number in political science or sociology or history—but not in literature. If, on the other hand, knowledge of the rights of women was necessary as a prelimi- nary to understanding either the meaning or the emotional or esthetic effect of Homer's art, that study did belong within that classroom and within the province of criticism. It was not, in that case, reductive. Similarly, any conclusions about the origins or backgrounds of Warren's work can be reductive. *All the King's Men* has been described as the best novel about the science of politics written in the twentieth century. It is, there- fore, a very legitimate subject of study for political scientists, but the novel has been reduced as a novel if the study ends with politics. As literature, the novel must be considered with regard to the artist's technical mastery of his materials, the effects and meanings he achieves by showing the psychological and dra- matic and spiritual relationships between groups and individu- als, the plotting of the complex forces that come to form a unified action or series of actions, and Jack Burden's intellectual and spiritual maturity as he comes to understand history and to be able to describe the facts and forces of history in the written word. These are aspects of criticism, and they are not reductive:

Writing is the process in which the imagination takes the place of literal living; by moving toward values and modifying, testing, and exfoliating older values. . . . I see the whole process as one of continu- ing experiment with values. . . .

But critics have to set up this contextual world in order to under- stand the writer in question. They do this in order for the reader to better understand the work of the writer in question. By setting up the contexts, the critics may come to *like* the writer less or may come to *like* him more. . . .

My notion of criticism is that its purpose is to deliver the reader back to the work. All the study *about* a writer or a work, all the analyses of background, of ideas, of the structure of a work—the purpose of all this is to prepare the reader to confront the work with innocence, with simplicity, with directness.[34]

Thus the critic may (perhaps usually does) move from the superficially appreciative, to the reductive, and, after analysis and thought, to the profoundly appreciative and comprehending. In some ways the critic's movement is an appreciative duplication of the artist's imaginative creation. Even Frost's poetry, Warren has said, "is a reported world. . . . But it is also a created world. It is, in other words, an image of the poet's vision of human fate—a vision of tenderness, courage, endurance, and delight mysteriously intertwined. In this sense, it is a manifestation of the deepest coherence, that of the poet himself who, in projecting the coherence of his created world, defines, even creates, the deeper coherence of the self." Then the reader, the critic, feels "an inner relation" to Frost's world and to him.[92]

There has been very little criticism of the origins and backgrounds, the milieu, of Warren's poetry. Students of Warren have been more philosophical than personal and lyrical. Studies of Warren's sources have been more concerned with the fiction than the poetry. His popular following has read him for his story-telling, his creation of his characters, his humor, and his handling of the American idiom. Those interested in literary genres and forms have occasionally read Warren within a historical and literary context. The religious and the philosophical and the political have read for his meaning. All of these components in similar fashion are found in other writers. A fallacy of literary history and of comparative study of literature is in finding the likenesses of literary artists. The proper study of literature is of its uniqueness. Much has been written about Warren. By his own admission his materials have come from history, which can be known to a great extent, and from his childhood and his community, which have been ignored as thoroughly as those of any major American writer. Truly for Warren there is a need to study how he has derived his poetry from life.

· 2 ·

The Penns,
The Warrens,
& the Boy

THE WESTWARD movement to an always hoped-for new Eden has been a constant in the history of America. It has dominated the lives of Robert Penn Warren's family and of his works. His ancestors, the Penns and the Warrens, traveled from Virginia to Kentucky, sometimes by way of North Carolina and Tennessee. Warren's own adventuresome migrations, first a few miles south to the literary center of Nashville, then to California, to Yale and Europe, to Louisiana and Minnesota, to Europe (especially France and Rome) again, and back again to Connecticut have been deeply symbolic in his life, in his concept of culture and history, and in his writings. Nearly all of his best literary works have been set meticulously in places and times and cultures he has known intimately, but except for *Night Rider* and a few short stories, the fiction has largely avoided the immediate locale of Guthrie and Todd County. Age and the changing of Warren's poetic talent have brought him back to his origins and the time of his youth.

Robert Penn Warren derives from a farming country family with more dignity and respect, I believe, than money and education. The lineage of the Warren family as they moved from Virginia southward and then to Kentucky in the nineteenth century is generally prolific and entangled—perhaps typical of the farming families who spread through the South, dying young, living long, marrying a second mate after the death of the first, building large families, creating numerous relationships and step relationships, earning a living, possessing enough to be warm and sufficiently country fed, passing the days in work and community relationships and sports afield. Warren once saw the Warren family Bible, but he has forgotten who may now have it. There are gaps in the statistical information as well as numerous hiatuses in accounts of the personal lives of these early Southern farming people. The history of a family in those times is more easily conjectured than it is found in documents.

The Warrens and the Penns drifted very early either down into North Carolina or into Tennessee and then moved back toward the north. (This was the pattern of those settlers who, Frank Lawrence Owsley discovered, followed isothermal zones as they stayed in geographical areas like those of their ancestors in Europe.) There was a Penn family in Virginia as early as 1621, and Warren's Penn ancestors moved from eastern to western Virginia when Patrick and Henry counties were first settled.[101] They came to Kentucky via Tennessee. But if the Warren family tree spreads out wide horizontally, the lineage of the Penns is tall and slender. Warrens had many homes in Trigg County; only one place was called the old Penn Place, and today the name has disappeared from the county.[81]

Warren's father once remarked to him that the family got to Kentucky around the War of 1812. Nancy Stuart and William H. Warren, the great grandparents of Robert Penn Warren, were married in Trigg County on Christmas day, 1838. Though only a laborer, William H. (1818-1864) could read and write. His bride, born in Virginia, could do neither, and so far no genealogist has been able to follow the trail of her family back over the mountains into the coastal state and to tell what Stuart line she belonged to. William H. Warren and Nancy had eight children, four boys and four girls. The oldest son, W.H.H. (sometimes referred to as W.H. Warren, Jr.), was the grandfather of Robert Penn. Born in Kentucky, December 12, 1839, he lived until January 12, 1893, twelve years before the birth of

Robert Penn Warren himself. His first wife, Sarah E. (1847-1877) was Warren's grandmother.

William H.H. Warren was described in the 1870 census as owning no land, and the value of his personal property was listed as three hundred dollars—a sum that might represent substantial possessions in those depressed Reconstruction times. His mother, Nancy Warren, lived next door to him with two daughters and two sons; three of these four aunts and uncles of Warren's father were listed in the census as farmworkers. Only one child, Julia, nine years old, was listed as not having an occupation. In Southern farm families of that time, children began full-time work around the age of twelve. Nancy Warren herself owned no farm and the census taker did not answer the question about her personal wealth.

Robert Franklin Warren, son of W.H.H. and Sarah E. and the father of Robert Penn Warren, was born in 1869. He was the second child. His mother died young, about a year after the birth of another child in 1876. In those days on the farm a man had to have a woman to help him, so W.H.H. Warren found Virginia or Jenny to be his wife and mother to his children; he "married the first girl down the road, as it was common to do in those days," his grandson says. W.H.H. himself died or became unable to support the family in his early fifties, leaving a wife and two sets of children unprovided for. The oldest son went west to Mexico and "made a good life for himself as a mining engineer."[43] He encountered Pancho Villa and returned to New Mexico, where shortly afterward he died of a wound, exposure, or natural causes, as his nephew remembers. He was buried in Albuquerque, and Robert Penn Warren remembers his father weeping when he heard the news—"a terrible sight" to the child.[58]

Robert Franklin Warren was fifteen or sixteen when his older brother fled to the West, leaving him to be the chief provider of their father's large household. Warren recalls that "my father never held a grudge against his brother for leaving him with a burden alone. They were in correspondence, and just now I remember something I had totally forgotten: My uncle sent my mother some rather fine rubies (fine, so I was told at the time,

I being very young then, say six or seven) to be made into a ring and a brooch. And after his brother was kicked out of Mexico by Pancho and died, my father and the widow were in fairly regular correspondence. When my uncle died, I now recall that my father sent her money, for when they had fled Mexico they got out with their hides. Later I remember a photograph sent him by the widow, this of her son, in a uniform of some military prep school."[95]

Denied his own ambitions by the needs of stepmother and brothers and sisters, Robert Franklin Warren received little formal education but made great efforts to learn on his own—a constant subject in the talk of his son and a theme in several literary works.[43] Robert Franklin's father owned a copy of *Paradise Lost* and "a lot of things like that." As a child Robert Penn found a copy of Dante (in English translation, probably Longfellow's) in the attic of the old Warren home. Warren was thus first introduced to Dante across a span of time by his ancestor's library. The usual rural Southerner did not take to ancient literatures in any language, and after Robert Franklin left home Jenny Warren threw away "a lot of things."[53] Warren's father wanted "to be a lawyer or a poet, and he wound up as the village banker."[43] But before rising to be a banker, he was a merchant, more likely a handyman and clerk in a country or small-town store.

Deprivations did not prevent Robert Franklin Warren's early study of poetry and languages, French and Greek and in his younger days he wrote several poems. Long afterward Robert Penn, by this time an author himself, found a book that contained some of his father's poems, but the father saw the book, took it from his son, and hid it or destroyed it—embarrassed, perhaps, by his early poetic efforts. The son remembered the book as being published about 1895 and containing poems by his father. Actually it was published in 1890, "edited and compiled under the supervision of Thos. W. Herringshaw." Called *Local and National Poets of America,* it must have been in part a vanity publication, and Robert Franklin perhaps paid for the printing of his own efforts.[99] At the time he was twenty-one years old; he had left his home and according to the five-line

biographical note was "clerking in a dry goods store" in Belle-
view, Kentucky. In a one-sentence sketch was a short summa-
tion of the interests of Robert Franklin Warren: "He is a great
lover of poetry and occasionally writes short poems, more for
recreation than fame." Well, perhaps he achieved the recreation
—the two poems he published did not deserve or attain fame.

OUR PILGRIMAGE

We are marching to that lovely land,
    Where saints are in power—children command;
Our feet are ever turned that way
    To lead us from this mortal fray.

Prestige of glory doth attract our sight,
    We are marching with the just, the right,
Our swift thought is our guide;
    We're walking with Jesus, side by side.

Lovely attractions have gone before;
    The ones that we love, the ones we adore.
Fond recollections to them doth fly;—
    We'll join them soon; yes, by and by.

'Tis the vision of Future that makes us true,
    And leads us upward from this land of dew;
Slowly we march to the heavenly portal
    Where all is truth, light, immortal.

Not as accomplished as an old-fashioned hymn perhaps, but
better than Julia A. Moore and certainly more deft than her
imitator in *Huckleberry Finn,* Emmaline Grangerford.

THE ORPHAN GIRL

Out upon the street in the cold.
    Goes our little wanderer,—
Lately from the dusty mold—
    The goods box yonder.

Her pitiful cries are heard
    All down Main street
And to the poor girl comes not a word
    From those she meets.

The stout, the wealthy, the great,—
  They all pass her by;
Nor will those of her own state
  Administer to her wailing sigh.

O think of the poor orphan girl!
  Her age is scarcely seven,—
Cast out in this dark world
  With naught to shelter her but heaven.

Her lot, oh it must be drear
  For one so delicate and small
To stand and not shed a tear
  As she watches the snowflakes fall.

What will be her fate?
  Ah, I readily see:
She will open the golden gate
  And quickly hide from thee.

By 1900 Robert Franklin Warren, still unmarried at thirty-one, had moved on to the relatively new commercial center of the railroad town of Guthrie, where he was working as a salesman. He had carried family responsibilities with him, and his eighteen-year-old brother, Ralph, was living with him almost as a son. Ralph had no occupation listed by the census taker, but he had attended school five months during the previous year. Single, looking after a younger brother, Robert Franklin had already recognized that his chance of success lay in property. He may have still been a great lover of poetry, but there is no indication that he still wrote poems—or proof that he didn't. He owned a house. Apparently his move from Cerulean to Guthrie was one of those countless migrations from a farm to a place of some commercial opportunity, this time a small town but a puffing railroad center.

Robert Franklin Warren's stepmother, Jenny Warren, was still living in Cerulean Springs, where the census of 1900 listed her as the head of a household with three children. Her occupation was listed as "N. G.," which might mean "not given." She could read, but she could not write. The same census listed Gabriel T. Penn, head of a family in Cerulean Springs all of

whom could read, and write. He owned a farm free of mort-
gages.

Gabriel Thomas Penn, Robert Penn Warren's maternal
grandfather, was the last head of a family that runs far back into
a haze of genealogical history and conjecture. All three of his
names belong to ancient American annals; he was at least the
fifth Gabriel in the family line in America and possibly the
fourth Thomas. Colonel Abram Penn, born in 1743, fought in
the Revolutionary War and was given a land grant around
Roanoke, Virginia; there he presided over the first court in
western Virginia in his clapboard house, called Poplar Grove.
He was a brother or first cousin of John Penn, a North Carolina
signer of the Declaration of Independence. Colonel Penn had
several sons who moved westward. One who moved to Tennessee was the grandfather of Gabriel Thomas, Warren's grandfather, born in 1836.[6]

Gabriel Thomas Penn married in Tennessee, had his first
child (James) in Tennessee in 1870, and apparently had to leave
there because of conflicts with guerrillas in the violent days of
Reconstruction. In 1881, he purchased from a family named
Goodwin an unspecified amount of land on the Muddy Fork of
the Little River in eastern Trigg County, Kentucky.[103] The following year, his wife's parents, J.T. and Mary A. Mitchell,
conveyed to him twenty-seven acres and thirty poles on the
Muddy Fork. The deed book names the price of the land as five
dollars, which in the language of deeds may mean that Gabriel
Thomas Penn bought acreage at a rather fair price (but paid
more than five dollars) or that it was given outright to the
younger couple.[102] By 1900 their daughter Ruth, who was to be
the mother of Robert Penn Warren, was twenty-four years old,
had finished her schooling, and was no longer at home. Before
she married she taught school in Hopkinsville. Two younger
daughters, Mary Mexico (named for a relative in the Mexican
War) and Sarah T., lived with the Penns. Apparently the Warrens and Penns, before the courtship and marriage of Ruth and
Robert Franklin, had only a speaking acquaintance.[43]

I have been unable to find any information about the courtship of Ruth Penn and Robert Franklin Warren, but the couple

married in 1904, settled into a home in Guthrie, and conceived a child. Robert Penn Warren was born at Third and Cherry in a little brick house (still standing today) one block west of the main street. Mary Warren and Thomas were born in other houses as the Warrens moved about, and Robert Penn's youth was spent "in the country surrounded by two or three acres" owned by his father.

Robert Penn Warren did not wish to be a boy of the town of Guthrie, but a country child of the county of Todd. The county was an older world. Put your hand east to west over the western part of a highway map of Kentucky, and it will cover much of what Warren came to regard as his childhood country. It is north of the Faulkner country in northern Mississippi, south of the lands of the midwestern writers, and it may be that some of the characteristics of both are apparent in the works of Warren. Your hand on the map will cover the confluences of all the great rivers that drain the waters from the eastern part of the United States into the Gulf of Mexico—the Ohio, the Cumberland, the Tennessee, and parts of the old Father of Waters himself. Westward are the Arkansas, the Missouri, and the Red River—those places toward which so many of Warren's characters looked and fled. Warren was not only a child of the South but also a product of central, agricultural America. His poems are based on this area.

Cerulean Springs

Robert Penn Warren spent most of his youthful summers at his grandfather Penn's farm near Cerulean Springs in Trigg County. The Penns were perhaps a little aristocratic and certainly aloof from the rest of the world. The old Penn Place is now remembered by that name by only a very few of the old people. (Hermit Mitchell says that only three people in Cerulean Springs in 1977 were also there when he moved there in 1919.)[77] The old home (torn down in 1975) was antebellum. It had not been built by the Penns, but when the grandson visited it, the family had lived there about half a century. It seemed almost as if they had established the place and built the house, with the wide boards that could have been sawed only from primeval and virgin forests. Round poles with the bark scaled off had been used as rafters to support the roof. The sills had been hewed out with an ax and fastened together with round wooden pegs. The rough large old bricks may have been made by the slaves of whatever family lived there before the Civil War. Even the ruins indicate that it was a comfortable place, but not one of the imposing homes scattered over what passed as the romantic, palatial South. It was only a short distance from the Muddy Fork stream and from the town and the resort or spa of Cerulean Springs (where the wealthy tourists of the day came to repose and impress). There was a mile-long vista over the fields and the pasture to the road that rushed suddenly up the hill to the old hotel.

Cerulean Springs began as a frontier town with the usual large number of saloons to slake the thirst of travelers and farmers, but it had become both a market village trading with the farmers and a spa ministering to high-society vacationers with the supposedly medicinal and certainly refreshing waters of mineral springs. In a guide to American spas published in 1927, Dr. William Edward Fitch described Cerulean Springs as on "a terminal spur of the Cumberland Range of Mountains, at an elevation of about 850 feet above sea level." The first hotel had been opened in 1819, but had burned in 1925. The owner promised a new "resort hostelry" for 250 guests by 1927, but it has never been built. Dr. Fitch listed ten mineral solids that might be medicinal and described the gases as "hydrogen sulphide, heavily charged." The Cerulean Springs water, he wrote, "is highly endorsed by the local profession in disorders of the stomach, kidneys and liver. There is sufficient sulphate ions in solution to exert mild laxative action with elimination of toxic poisons from the bowels and blood. Prof. Herman Schlundt, Department of Chemistry, Columbia University, has tested the water and found it to possess marked radioactivity."[98]

So the tourists of those days of Warren's childhood visits came to improve their health and to promenade. There were several stores in the town. It was a resort, one old-timer says,

for "people from all over." Warren remembers that his youngest aunt, Sarah, who took care of old Captain Penn, met her
husband-to-be at a dance in the outdoor dancing pavilion of the
hotel. For the time the Cerulean Hotel was elaborate and luxuri-
ous; it had one hundred guest rooms, a skating rink, a bowling
alley, a dance pavilion with a skating area around it, live bands.
Once a large postmasters' convention was held there. Fine china
with a portrait of the Cerulean Springs Hotel on each of the
pieces was made in Germany and shipped to this resort set in
the midst of the back country of the farming South. Hermit
Mitchell remembers that he had delivered seventeen hundred
pounds of ice to the hotel on the day that it burned, the last
Saturday night of August, 1925.

During the summers of his boyhood Robert Penn Warren
and his Grandfather Penn seldom journeyed the long hot mile
to the little town of Cerulean Springs, where Uncle Cortez
Warren was running a store and the stepgrandmother, Jenny
Warren, lived in one of the houses of the village. Gabriel
Thomas kept his family on the farm, receiving very few visitors
and not visiting anyone.

In Robert Penn Warren's poems he writes about his family,
the country people, and some of the people of the town—but
not of the hotel, nearby but hidden by the terrain and the trees;
in his poems he ignored the hotel as Faulkner ignored the state
university in Jefferson. Certainly he had no social yearnings in
his heart, living with his grandfather, a big, bearded, self-sufficient man, "a man, too, who had an old-fashioned contempt for
town-folks (land was all)."[95] Gabriel Thomas Penn permitted
no one outside the family to come onto his place. His grandson
says that he was "totally cut off from the rest of the world."[39]
Relatives came, and twice each summer the Rawls family, "two
daughters and a son, my only playmate," came "for late Sunday
dinner." The older daughter had studied "elocution," and she
recited some of Gabriel Thomas Penn's favorite poems "with
gestures and stances."[5] When the Penn family went to church,
Gabriel Thomas and his kin left immediately afterward and
drove off without chatting with anyone. For the boy it was an
isolated world. Almost daily Robert Penn retreated to the

woods. He had almost no playmates. "I'd see a white boy once every month, maybe."[43]

Only a long time after the summers at Grandfather Penn's did Warren realize that there was something "peculiar" about his grandfather. He never "talked about his own life. Only objective things. For instance, I know about the guerrilla stuff (as it affected him in making him go to Kentucky) only from his sister-in-law, my Great-Aunt Anna, an old lady I was very fond of." In the poem "Court-Martial," though, all that the boy ever learns of his grandfather's killing of the bushwhackers is told to him by the grandfather himself. Close as the boy and his Grandfather Penn were, talkative as the old man was, bound up in family ties as much as he was, Gabriel Thomas Penn did not talk to the youth about the Penn family and the boy's ancestry.

What I knew, including the picture of my great-grandfather Mitchell (an impressive old Scotch-Irishman who looks ten feet tall with a long black coat and big gold watch chain and white beard and a dour Presbyterian face like Stonewall, with a hand going far down to lie on the shoulder of wife number what) I got from my great-aunt, one of his daughters. I let time get away without finding out a thousand facts I'd like to know. The last time I saw my Aunt Sarah (in Florence, when Eleanor and I were living at the Rocca in Tuscany and had driven over to see her, to show off our "git"—anyway, I was crazy about her) I tried to get her on a few matters, but the time and place weren't right. Not that she was hesitant. I never saw her again, though we were always in correspondence. I kept meaning to go down to Florida to see her, but time slipped away. She had with her a red-headed young grandson, about twelve or fourteen I guess, and said to me: "See I just can't do without another little red-headed boy. They're the kind I like." Then kissed boy and me. I used to think that the fact of my ignorance was merely that I had been too young—and I was, no matter how interested I was in their other talk. But anyway, maybe the War closed the mouth of some.[95]

On his grandfather's farm Warren was often alone with the July flies, the daily heat, the night sounds of the fields, and the sunset or dawn racket of several hundred guinea fowl that prowled the woods but roosted near the house. "I have the image of my grandfather sitting under a cedar tree, his chair propped against the tree, a pipe in his mouth, a stick across his lap, and myself a child nearby, and some scratching on the ground. He would have been scratching the strategy of some battle, from the Civil War or something."[23] With white hair, "a rather pointed beard, blue jean pants, a black tie and an open collar, he was a striking relic." Using cartridge shells, he and the boy drew the strategies and movements of Civil War troops and of Napoleon in the dust of the farm. Grandfather told the boy stories of Shiloh, of an event at Fort Pillow, and of the war in northern Mississippi.[5]

The days with his grandfather gave Warren a background for his Agrarian beliefs and may have a lot to do with Warren's never having allowed a television set in his home. Gabriel Thomas Penn humorously acknowledged only two benefits from the modern world—"fly screens" and "painless dentistry." About sixty years later in an interview on educational television, the grandson added, "and I think he was right."[47] And the grandfather abetted Warren's mother and father in urging—if any urging was necessary—the boy to read.

The Southern talent for narrative and poetic speech may begin very early with talk between parent and child, between grandparent and child. There was talk on the farm, talk in Cerulean and Guthrie, talk during the midday hours when it was too hot to work, and talk during the long hours after supper while the sun went down and the family waited for bed. Gabriel Thomas Penn and Robert Penn Warren talked. When Warren visited in Cerulean, the war was only half a century past, and its effects and memories still survived and were to survive even through the First World War and until 1920. So old man and young talked of the War and the times and man.

Both grandfathers—W.H.H. Warren was now long dead—had fought with Forrest and in the battle of Shiloh. Grandfather Penn was a captain of cavalry. A contradictory rumor persists that he was promoted to captain at Shiloh and told to raise his own company.[51] Grandfather Warren was a captain and then a major. A great uncle was shot in the leg.[35] Captain Penn served in the Fifteenth Tennessee Cavalry as commander of Company H.[100] On March 10, 1864, Captain Warren com-

manded six companies of Colonel Forrest's regiment. They
were sent to Marion County, Alabama, "to protect the foun-
dries, &c., against tories and deserters."[104] Major Warren sur-
rendered his command on May 9, 1865, near Courtland,
Alabama, without asking the permission of his superior—probably because of the chaos of the end of the war. Whether the
two grandfathers of Robert Penn Warren knew each other during the war is entirely a matter of speculation. Considering the
relatively high rank of both, it is likely. Warren was then a
citizen of Trigg County, but Penn moved to Trigg after the war,
when he had created a number of enemies in Tennessee by
hanging terrorist bushwhackers who were neither Confederate
nor Yankee and who were engaged in killing and stealing. Even
when Captain Penn and Major Warren became citizens of the
same county, it is unlikely that they were ever close acquaintances, because of the isolation of the Penn family. Family
"chatter," Warren remembers, tells that James Penn (the only
son of Gabriel Penn) and Robert Franklin Warren were friends
in boyhood or young manhood. But "the Penns and the Warrens never exchanged visits," Warren says; "in fact my grandfather would see only one family in Cerulean except on business
in my time."[95]

Soldier, officer, and hanger of bushwhackers, the older Penn
had been violently involved in the conflict, but he was "opposed to slavery." And also opposed to secession. Though in a
border state, he was bred a loyal Southerner. But like a certain
number of Southerners, particularly those with strong Virginia
ties, they felt that "they" had made the Union. He would have
said that "the world doesn't work by ethical standards, the
world works the way it can, and this will change."[95] (Saying
this a half century after those old conversations, was Warren
explaining truly the views of his grandfather, or was he putting
his later literary themes in the old man's mouth, or were the two
the same? Did the theme come from the ancestor?) Because of
his views he was "at odds with the neighbors," but "when the
time came, he was on horseback," and he was with his people
as soon as the North invaded Virginia.[47] In wartime, he said,
"You went with your people."[6]

At first Warren says (and here he may look back to the past and see how his later profound attitudes toward violence were even in these times beginning to build):

It's all very romantic because he [the boy] doesn't understand blood, but I do remember very distinctly the shock of discovering that the old man, my grandfather, who had fought battles, wasn't romantic about it. I remember that shock very distinctly. It was a story, an important story to tell, but it wasn't romantic. This was a great shock, because I wanted to make it all very romantic in my childish way. This shock was quite real. I even wrote a poem about it, called "Court-Martial" —about that moment when the old man was not romantic at all, and I had been romantic, and suddenly he was realistic about it. So it carries a double thing with it. Though any defeated society is going to romanticize its war, that was done by the U.D.C., not the old men.[35]

The war had not been romantic for Captain Penn. He and his men had not only fought with hot lead and cold steel, but had been hangers of bushwhackers. "Both sides," Warren says, "were hanging without much trial. My grandfather said they gave them a fair trial, it just didn't take very long." But Captain Penn's property in Tennessee was confiscated, as the boy heard, and families of the guerrillas placed murder charges against him. So he moved to Kentucky, making Robert Penn Warren the grandson of four Kentucky grandparents.[43]

Grandfather Penn quoted literature—"Byron and Scott and poems like 'The Turk Lay in the Guarded Tent.' "[26] He "recited poetry by the yard"; he quoted Fitz-Greene Halleck, Burns, and "some Pope and bits of Shakespeare floating around."[52] Warren's father and his maternal grandfather "had books everywhere." The uncles and aunts would say, "Poppa is an inveterate reader," and little Robert Penn thought they were saying "Confederate."[39] He read history (Egyptian, Confederate, American). But there was no one in the community to talk with about his reading except his visiting grandson.

To his grandson, then and later enamored of history, he was "the living symbol of the wild action and romance of the past."[26] Lack of economic or worldly success gave him more time with his thoughts and his books, and with his grandson.

He was a tobacco farmer for a time and a tobacco buyer. With tobacco on consignment, he forgot to pay a premium and a warehouse burned.[52] An honorable but impractical man, his grandson says,[5] he refused to go bankrupt and "stuck by his debt and paid it off . . . but that took a long time and set him back deeply. But that's why they called him a visionary."[43] Warren's mother too was a reader and an encourager of reading, and the only old maid aunt, "paradoxically the beauty in the family," kept Warren from his outdoor play until he had finished his algebra and Latin.

Once when Warren was visiting his Grandfather Penn he was working in the tobacco fields, dropping or setting plants. An old man was

working there—a lot of people, hired hands, . . . working with the sharecroppers, and this was a hired man, an old man named Mac something (a Scots name), and he was mighty mean to me all day long. He kept teasing me in a nasty kind of a way, and finally he says, "You're the kind of a little son of a bitch who thinks that the world's round, aren't you? You've been to school, haven't you?" And I said, "Well, isn't it round?". . . "Oh, you've been at school, you're so proud of yourself. . . . You don't know who I am?" I said, "No, I don't." He said, "Well, I'm your Grandmother Jenny's father," and this was the only time I ever saw him or heard of him. He was—he was saying—the father of my father's stepmother. . . . My father's stepmother's father. . . . He was working as a hired hand on my Grandfather Penn's place. Nothing was said about this; . . . that's the only time I ever heard of him. And I never said a word about it. Why—I don't know.[53]

And Robert Franklin Warren supported or helped to support Jenny Warren all the rest of her life.

The encounter between the narrow and ignorant old man and the learned but innocent boy echoed a great controversy of that time—the Scopes trial was to come a few years later in Tennessee. The Apostle John said that the world had four corners; for one it was the authority of the Bible, for the other the learning he had encountered in books and the assumptions of his family. It was the conflict too between the country laborer for hourly wages and the casual child worker who could quit with the first pain or an early sweat, between the hired and the hirer. The moment must have been one of stress and bewilderment for the red-headed little boy in the tobacco field, away from his town-resident parents, and puzzling over the animosities that exist in the world and the complexities of in-law and step and distant and strange family relationships. Warren has written no poem about the incident. But who is to tell how many of his poems are based on characters in that sort of conflict and incidents of that stark and angry abruptness?

Guthrie

Warren's summers with the Penns during his childhood were isolated rural times; for most of the year he lived in Guthrie, among children of workers and men of commerce, in a town with no Southern past, indeed with almost no past at all, for the town of Guthrie had been spawned by the L&N railroad.

An old inn had been started on a route where the stagecoaches headed for the West; near Spring Creek, close to Guthrie, Spottswood Smith, of Virginia, and about a dozen others, had settled in 1814-1815; about four families came in 1820, and there had been a store in the area as early as 1821.[96] But as late as 1844, what is now known as Guthrie was "a stopping place called Pondy Woods, two miles east of Graysville."[97] The first trains steamed through in 1868, and a landowner, J.C. Kendal, laid out a town, named Guthrie for the president of the railroad and a member of Congress; two lines crossed there in 1870 and hopes of development rose.[96] It was almost as if the Southern rural earth divided like the Red Sea and a new land, the town of Guthrie, was set down in the middle of the swamp and the farmland of the Red River and Cumberland River valleys.

The old farm families remained surrounding the town, and they traded in the town, but whatever survived of the old Southern culture when the railroad came gave way to the new world, a nondescript culture, and a small town without the marks of the other towns of the time and place. Warren has recently written that Guthrie was "anything but the usual older Southern town, being on the order of a real estate project, having been put there when two railroads crossed. The only hope that the L&N would put a roundhouse there or do something equally wonderful came to nothing; and after a period as a fairly prosperous little market town . . ., it is now moribund with half the houses unoccupied."[95] Guthrie was still living on hope when Warren was born in 1905, but the ambition began to wane slowly as time drew on into the twentieth century. It was, as Warren says, "one long downhill drag."

Guthrie magniloquently claimed to be the "crossroads of railroads in America," and a lot of trains did stop there. In fact it was said that only one train ever passed directly through Guthrie without a pause—the one that carried a fire engine to Clarksville, Tennessee, when that town burned.[79] There was a crosstie plant at Guthrie, and it treated ties for a wide area of the South. There was a broom plant that shipped several carloads a week. It was a center of commerce set in the midst of farming country, a new place for most of its residents, a town "without a sense of belonging in any particular place or having any particular history."[7]

Warren has said that the population of Guthrie when he was born in 1905 was about "1500, more or less,"[26] but the figure is too large. Dun and Bradstreet (September, 1905) lists it as 807 and describes the town as "A Banking Town." There were about forty businesses, of the usual types found in a country town. Besides the seventeen grocery and drygoods stores, there were five saloons, two publishers, an electric lighting plant, an "opera house" with real plays, two restaurants, and a combination grocery store and undertaker. By 1910, that weird combination had gone out of business, and in that year and 1915 one business firm provided furniture and funerals. The county seat of Elkton, an old settlement, looked on Guthrie as a rough town, filled with transients. There was cockfighting, and even the mayor, it is said, controlled four or five bootleggers. Newspapers in Kentucky wrote of Guthrie as a town noted for violence. One old-timer has vivid memories of past blood-letting. "You wouldn't believe the people in my lifetime that have been killed in this town. Shot. Cut up. Doctors come in here and stay overnight and say they've seen more blood than they've ever seen in their life."[62] "It was a violent world," Warren has written.

Our nearest neighbor, Judge Kimbrough, had killed a man or was reported to have done so. William White, a man-size big boy, in 10th grade, killed a carnival hand one night in a fight with *tent-pegs,* was tried for murder and acquitted, and came back to school just afterwards. [See also *Jefferson Davis,* p. 18.] Some of the schoolyard fights were serious (I remember some of the railroad boys carried heavy nuts used to bolt rails together as weapons). Before Mrs. Muirhead became principal (when war came), there was usually a physical fight between the biggest boy in high school and the new principal. I saw Mr. Willett (a frail, thin, Ichabod Crane sort of man, just out of U. of K.—M. A., I think) throw Charlie Parham (who outweighed him by 50 pounds) through the glass of a high window & down nearly a story to hard ground—Charlie was threatening him, and wouldn't take his seat. But Charlie was good-humored. The next day he said: "I tried him and he was faster than I was. When I hit the ground I hit running; I thought he might be following." Mr. Willett had just calmly gone back to business. "Next, please." [Compare this story to a variant in *Jefferson Davis,* p. 17.]

The assistant principal that year (this I did not see) was assaulted at band practice by a big boy named Weinstein. The boy used an iron poker and the intended victim caught the blow and hit the assailant on his head with a piano stool. The father of the boy sued the assistant principal, who was acquitted in Elkton, and had no more trouble. Never challenged again—his name, I recall, was William Barker.

The air of violence continued (not in school) even after World War II. My brother's brother-in-law, Thomas and I were sitting over drinks one night at the brother-in-law's farm—a lonesome place—and a Negro came in to say that somebody was stealing corn (very valuable then). So Felix, wordlessly, went to his gun room, handed each of us an automatic shotgun or rifle, and said, "Let's go." I mentioned the sheriff to Felix—and he said, "Hell, he's ten miles away and we're here."[95]

Guthrie is built on the Tennessee and Kentucky state line. And right on the line was what they called "niggertown"; Squiggtown was its name. A combination liquor store (Tennessee) and grocery store (Kentucky) was built on the state line, so that a fugitive could escape arrest by running from one end of the building to the other. At the railroad station a big old-fashioned hotel thrived on the business of renting rooms and serving meals to travelers during stopovers while they waited to change trains. "At the hotel," Warren remembers, "was a newsstand where one could buy a *Nation, New Republic, Poetry, Dial* and such—in the early 1920's." One woman in Cerulean Springs, somewhat younger than Warren, remembers how she rode the train to college many times, stopped in Guthrie on Sunday night, and often ate dinner at the hotel with Mr. and Mrs. Robert Franklin Warren. It was a place to get through.

In some ways Todd County was a mixture of three cultures: the rich old plantation past of the Cumberland valley and aristocratic small cities like Clarksville twelve miles away over the Tennessee line, the new commercial town struggling to become a transportation center, and the small farmers to the north in the Cumberland hills east of the county seat of Elkton. The variety of cultures and of economic systems in a small geographical area may be in part responsible for Warren's knowledge of widely variant Southern ways of life as well as his lack of a strong loyalty to any one kind of Southernism. Some white farmers moved from the mountains to become small farmers in the lowlands. Though Warren lived and played in the town, he turned more to the country when he could. Those marvelous sketches (usually short) in his poetry and his fiction of the small farmer derive, it is said, from Warren's quiet and close childhood observation of the country at Cerulean and especially of the countrymen who came to Guthrie to trade. He saw country people like Ashby Wyndham in *At Heaven's Gate,* Jeff York in "The Patented Gate and the Mean Hamburger," and Milt Alley's family in "Blackberry Winter" and "A Christmas Gift." Warren does not know the real Southern dirt farmer as well as Faulkner did, but no other prominent Southern writer does. On Saturdays when the farmers came to town to trade Warren sat around and listened to them talk and talked to them himself.[82]

From one perspective the life of Warren in Guthrie was something like an idyll of Tom Sawyer or the exciting and happy escapades of the adventurous Faulkner brothers in Mississippi, with home-made toys and vehicles, practical jokes, fox and dog races, and the vigorous games of masculine childhood. Diagonally across what was later to become a street from the Warrens lived Kent Greenfield's family in "a rather large farm house—more farm house than town house" placed in a way to create a street corner. Kent was Warren's favorite childhood playmate and possibly the most constant friend Warren had in Guthrie. In an early grade he sent Kent a Christmas card he had made himself. "It showed a picture of Santy Claus looking at his ledger. On the left the heading was 'Bad Boys', and on the right 'Good Boys.' Kent's name headed the 'Good Boys.' " Many years later, when Warren was in his early fifties, "Kent sent me the same old card, which he had kept all these years, with a one sentence note: 'Please send back.' I sent it back."[95]

Warren—three grades ahead of himself in school and forced to cope with boys older and bigger than he—emphasized the physical in order to survive, first, and then in later years to meet the requirements of those well-rounded young men who wished to become Rhodes scholars. As a child he first swam in the pond where clay had been dug up for brick.[62] Later he could jump into the river and swim three or four hours while carrying on a conversation.[63] He even bought a book on swimming.[66] After a swim, he would leap into the road and jog back to Guthrie for six or seven miles.[63] "Lord, I couldn't stay out of the water," Warren recollected to David Farrell. "I was mad for the water and still am, and even if it was cold I'd be in it trying to be . . . a lumberman on a log and, oh, things like that. . . . My first years, they finally took me out just for safety's sake."[49] He swam in a pond and a stream in the Cumberland valley—Red River—which Warren has called a "mixed country, fine rolling farmland breaking here and there into barrens, but with nice woodlands and plenty of water, a country well adapted to the proper pursuits of boyhood."[26] He took walks of six or seven miles. Lester Lannom says that he could outswim, outrun, outwalk anyone in Guthrie. Once he ran to swim in the Red River, swam for three hours, and then ran home when he finished.[74]

In a reminiscence written when Warren was in his early seventies, he had a rather mild, ordinary, and perhaps a little forgetful recollection of his childhood:

I often had "friends" in to play in the ordinary way. And the childish baseball games were usually in the open spaces above our house (which belonged to my father). In the day-to-day way I didn't feel isolated, but occasionally there'd be some episode of "persecution" almost always stopping short of any violence. But there were things that made me aware of differences in general attitude. Richard Bourne and I played chess (having taught ourselves from handbooks and books of "problems.") My interest in "natural history"—prowling the countryside for specimens for collections—was something entirely outside the common run of activity. You went to the woods to hunt or swim—period. The fact of the routine of study and the wilful reading was generally regarded as, at the best, a little nutty. I had a chemical laboratory—poor thing it was, too, and in a boyish way fooled with that. My father bought me a ten volume set of electrical handbooks (too advanced for me on the whole) but I managed to build a radio that worked by the barest. I would have been an even bigger fool than I was if I hadn't realized some difference between my interests (boyish and trivial as most were) and the world around me. And the kind of woods-prowling that Kent and I did just for the hell of it, sometimes with air rifle or .22.[95]

The Warren boys, Robert Penn and Thomas, did little farm-work. Their father was not a farmer, and they had no relatives near Guthrie who were farmers. They may have helped to thresh wheat once or twice, and farming went on in the countryside all around Guthrie. Robert Penn sometimes worked on his grandfather's farm in Cerulean at the usual wage—when he wished to (RPW on ms.). He took a course in manual training when he attended school in Clarksville. Without the obligation of a great deal of physical labor, Warren resorted to exercise. Lester Lannom says that Warren knew you must cultivate both mind and body. "Unconscious of himself as a person," Warren was self-effacing, whether he ran or swam or what. Even with all this Tarzan-like exertion, books came first. "I don't imagine he was the type that would have too many close friends until he had finished his academic" studies. The physical and the studious in his personality were reconciled, according to Lester Lannom, by Warren's superior character. "Robert Penn Warren never had a feeling of superiority; he held Guthrie in highest esteem, never looked down on anyone in his entire life. He was never a loner except he had a driving ambition to accomplish and he did accomplish it." The praise is so unreserved that it may cast doubt on itself: "The simplicity of his life is what impressed me more than anything else after he got to be famous" and "he wore blue jeans before it got to be acceptable in Guthrie."[74]

Warren's childhood friend Richard Bourne had a rifle, and he and Warren shot bullfrogs. On several nights they went frog gigging, and on one of them they gigged twenty frogs, cut off the legs, and threw the frogs away.[66] Richard's mother or aunt fried the frog legs for the boys' breakfast. They were interested in the way the frog legs jumped as they were fried in the pan. Years later in 1956 Warren used the image of the jumping legs to describe the Fugitives assembled at their reunion with onlookers watching them jump as they read their poetry. Warren picked blackberries, fished, rode horseback, hunted arrowheads, caught butterflies and mounted them between sheets of glass.[62] Anticipating his long poem on Audubon, he studied the beauty of the birds, perhaps puzzling over the beauty in death and the awful loss of life in the bird. He became something of an amateur taxidermist. Kent Greenfield, in the woods with Warren, mocked bird calls before his voice changed.[72]

One summer when Warren had just turned seventeen, he went to Fort Knox and worked through military training in a program intended to train late teen-agers for a month for each of four summers. ("A few couldn't take it and left," Warren says. "I'd have died first.") While enlisted in this Civilian Military Training Camp (CMTC), he wrote his first poem and published it in the camp paper at Fort Knox. He hunted a bit, especially with Kent Greenfield, for small game—nothing on the scale of Ike McCaslin and Faulkner in the Big Woods of Mississippi. They shot whatever ran or flew by. In the woods and fields he studied the natural world and collected things. Later he remembered that he had not been "civilized enough for

vivisection (that is, I retained a primitive pity for the bird during its life)."[88] He was an avid collector of Indian artifacts,
Everett Frey says, especially at the ages of seven, eight, and
nine. He found not only arrowheads but also tomahawks, mill-
stones, and tools.

Warren was active in sports even if he did not excel. In
school athletics, odds were against him from the first—a frail
boy three grades ahead of his years. At sixteen he weighed 116
or 117, and he was about five feet eight or nine. He played
baseball in pick-up games and says that, being the owner of a
catcher's mitt, he had to catch for Kent Greenfield, "this guy
who pitched for the New York Giants and I'd be fifty feet
behind the plate."[54] He played all the children's games that
were familiar in a time of home made toys and unsupervised
play. He rode stick horses, played kick-the-can, rushed about
in cowboy and Indian warfare. As small children Warren and
his playmates made trains out of shoeboxes tied together with
strings, with holes in the sides and lights to make the boxes look
like railroad cars.[70] Warren's father gave him masks, foils, and
a handbook, and he and Richard Bourne practiced fencing.[95]
Warren had a basketball goal at his house, an unusual possession in Guthrie. In later years he and Everett Frey even played
a few games of tennis.[70]

A major enterprise among the children in Warren's neighborhood was the building and excavating of rooms and tunnels
and underground structures of various kinds. To hear the talk
of the old people who did the digging as children, one would
think that anyone who walked in a backyard near the Warrens'
was in danger of falling into a cavern. The children built a house
in the Warrens' chicken yard, a sort of big underground play-
house, which they "played in all the time."[58] In the old wornout
joke, Warren said they were digging to China.[76] They built a
subterranean passage back of the garden and had a sort of
shelter,[70] an underground cabin with two or three rooms
boarded up with planks to hold the dirt over the roof.[61] There
was a trench and a dugout like those used in World War I. [70]
One of the boys had a .22 pistol, and it fell out of his pocket
while they were playing leapfrog. After that, Ruth Warren did

not allow her son to play with that boy any more. (On the other hand, she did not object to rifles used for shooting in the woods and fields.) Once a man fell into the boys' diggings and became entangled in all the things they had carried into their hideout. Ruth Warren helped the man get out, and then she threw the junk into the trash can. She was firm enough to make the boys "step about."[76]

Warren, then, was an outdoorsman even though in athletics he was untalented and too young and small. In walking, running, swimming, roaming the woods and fields, where size was not a decisive factor, he could hold his own. "I had a rather friendless boyhood in one sense," Warren has said. "I played a lot with other boys, but I had only two or three good friends. My childhood really was tied with the country, not the town. I loathed the town. I couldn't wait to get out of it and loved to go to the country. Often I spent whole days out in the woods. I used to go in a buggy with one of the country boys for nutting or hunting."

Warren did not begin "to get his growth" until late, probably nineteen. At twenty, he remembers, he was a little under six feet and "thickening out." His normal weight was over 180 by the 1940s (when he was regularly at the gymnasium for basketball, track, weights). In later years he has retained his physical condition. He still wears suits of the 1940s—being, he says, "a man to hang on to clothes." The coat of a blue suit he was married in (1952) has long since become a blue blazer, and it still fits. For years he has swum a kilometer before breakfast in his big pool in Vermont plus an hour of outdoor work or hiking or clambering.[95]

If Warren was beneath the average in some physical accomplishments, he was unsurpassed in the activities of the mind that were available in Guthrie. He learned to read from a book in an incident that involved "my favorite poem. That was 'Horatius at the Bridge' by Macaulay." His father read to the children every night, and he was forced to read "Horatius" over and over. And finally he just rebelled. "Kindly man, but rebelled. And he says, 'Take the book and read it. You can read it already.' "[48] So Warren read the long narrative poem at six.

By nine he had advanced to Browning's "How They Brought the Good News from Ghent to Aix." When he was thirteen or fourteen his father gave him *The Origin of Species* and *The Descent of Man.* Also he read the long and complex *History of Civilization in England* by Henry Thomas Buckle.[27] He read some Conrad when he was fifteen or sixteen but does not believe that Conrad had any significant influence on his own work.[95] In high school he wrote a report on *Lord Jim,* and he also read *The Duchess of Malfi.*[66] His real introduction to poetry came, he says, in trying to write a term paper in the Guthrie High School on "Lycidas." "I never understood it," he says, but it hit him "in the gut." He read Bulwer-Lytton, Cooper, Thackeray, and Dickens, Ouida, and so forth, he says, "before I discovered to my delight the Boy Scout Books." He read "Thrillers, detective stories, a lot of poetry, Macaulay, and Gibbon, and a good deal of American history"—almost whatever came to hand in the libraries at his father's and grandfather's homes and at school.[107] After reading the Darwin, he turned to Tarzan. He owned every book written by Edgar Rice Burroughs, who had published twenty-eight novels (besides twenty-one others in magazines) in 1920 by the time Warren was fifteen. Always his grades were so good that the other children looked on him as a teacher's pet and many disliked him and abused him for that reason. After he became older, one of his contemporaries said, "he wasn't any fun." He stayed inside and read, "and that's never very good."[58]

It was a little early for dating, but even before Warren went to college at Vanderbilt when he was sixteen, he was interested in girls. Some people about his age say Warren never had a date in Guthrie at all,[65] and in a mature sense of the term perhaps he did not. But neighbors did not keep constant watch, and there were a few (Warren believes "one") awkward (Warren says "awfully" awkward) beginnings at trying to date the girls while Warren was fifteen in Guthrie. Once when he was about sixteen he dated a girl and made only the comment that she was "an amiable girl."[73] Others say he was too young to have a girl friend before he went to college at such an early age.[62] Once two girls scratched his face badly even though they liked him very much, but they could not stand his high grades in his school work.[65] Mrs. Hugh B. Disharoon, now of Hopkinsville, remembers that she had one date with Warren when she lived in Guthrie, but she says, "I don't think it was his idea at all." As she remembers it they did not have a lot in common and Warren left perhaps as early as nine o'clock. They sat in a swing on the front porch and "let it go back and forth till we got worn out from swinging and he went home. That's not the normal approach, but it's what we had."[59] That was fifty or sixty years ago, and Mrs. Disharoon cannot remember what they talked about. Red haired and freckle-faced, Warren could not have attracted with his good looks. But he did date more than one girl. Mrs. Dorothy McElwain, of Elkton, remembered in 1977 that she had had dates with young Warren when he was six- teen. He "flaunted that he was smart." He talked about the sky, the stars, the moon. He was so far ahead of her, she says, that "she felt that she was in the dark."[75]

The girl regarded by several as the "Elizabeth Taylor of Guthrie" says that Warren was "odd and not popular."[68] As he passed by on the street, people would greet him as "Pret-tee Red." If they called him that, Warren says he never heard it. Richard Bourne says that Warren was frail, bookish, that he had the reputation of effeminacy, that he was called a sissy, that he was kept close at home while he was in town but was allowed to ramble away in the woods, taught at home (the Warren children were required "to study five nights a week") that he was "kind of distant."[63]

In his study of Whittier, Warren wrote that "Almost every- one has an Eden time to look back on, even if it never existed and he has to create it for his own delusion."[15] In part childhood (at least in his private activity) might have been Warren's Eden time (or the early days of his second marriage), but if it was, he did have to create a good many of the glories for himself in his middle teens. He remembers chiefly the good times he had alone or with a couple of friends.[95]

Warren's was an extreme example of a brilliant boy pushed ahead of himself physically and perhaps emotionally in the interest of his intellectual potentialities. His attributes were

contradictory, and it is no wonder that he remembers the summers on the farm with his grandfather in Cerulean as among the
happiest and most adjusted days of his life. As a schoolboy in
Guthrie, Warren endured the trials of the damned.

His contemporaries say that he brought strange lunches to
school, not the big white insufficiently cooked biscuits and ham
or syrup of the other children, but a can of English peas, or
tomatoes, or corn. Warren calls the story of the lunches a "*plain
lie.*" Another story recounts that a boy gave him part of a
sandwich without telling him what it was, and Warren believed
it was the most delicious sandwich he had ever eaten in his life.
The boy told him it was a "shit sandwich," and Warren has-
tened home after school to ask his mother to make him one. He
was, the story says, too innocent to know the meaning of the
word. Warren told me in 1979 that the whole story is "just a
plain lie. A totally, totally, totally plain lie. . . . I don't remember
the time when I didn't know the word *shit.*" He laughed: "I
knew the word *shit* pretty well."[95] And two years later he
added, "Shit on them."

A similar story, much more widely circulated than that of the
sandwich is about a hanging—or two. His fellows tied a rope
around him and hanged him in a well. One says the rope was
around his neck.[60] Another reports that he was hanged in a well
or cistern, "suspended," as he called it. Warren was hollering
for help, and someone came along and got him out. Nothing
was ever done about it. Warren "took it and had guts."[65] In
another version (or perhaps even another incident or another
erroneous memory) Warren was taken into a barn by some
boys, who put a rope around his neck, threw it over a rafter,
pulled it up, and "about pretty near hanged him." (Curiously,
this story is told by one of the same persons who told the story
about the hanging in the well. The variations in the stories
probably indicate something happened but also add to the
doubt of their authenticity.)[61] Again, somebody came by and
scared off the boys.

Warren has written his version: "There is one piece of truth
here. Once some older and bigger boys got me in a deserted
building, maybe a barn, and put a rope around my neck and

started pulling on it. They said they'd teach me about grade-making. They lifted me off my toes two or three times, to scare me. Then one of them, suddenly, got ashamed, or sick of what they were doing, and made them quit. Later one or two tried to apologize and I said, 'Go to hell.' That is the *one* story of all the real persecution stories. I was lucky—I seriously considered shooting the ring-leader to death, then thought of the family trouble."[95]

The first time I told this story of the hanging to Warren he could not remember it at all. After almost two years and twice reading my account he did remember and write me the account quoted above. That he did after some time recall the terrifying event from the past and tell the details of his memory lends credence to his version of his life in Guthrie and suggests that the talk in the town has often been substantially exaggerated even when it contains some truth.

Old timers also recall that if a boy walked from school with a roll of music in his hand, he was "beat up" before he reached town.[65] It was against the custom to study, and one boy who was a good student made the others look bad. Ruth Warren ordered Robert Penn to bring his books home from school, and one other boy was given the same instructions. Someone knocked the books out of their hands and all over the sidewalk. Everyone laughed. Then a group kicked the books on out into the street. Warren says that the story was "Not possible! The line from school was monitored, and the students were checked to see that they carried books home."[95] Whatever really happened—if anything—the roughnecks thought of it as a sport rather than a cruelty.

The Guthrie schools had outdoor privies, necessarily with many holes to accommodate the rush of a lot of students in a short time during recess. One of the boys' diversions was to hold a boy by his feet and lower his head down into the pit of the toilet. Warren is said to have fallen victim to this form of entertainment too. They held him far enough down to make the experience as nauseous as it could be without any actual physical contact between the boy and the waste. As the story goes, Warren just endured the unpleasantry until the boys had

finished having what they thought was their merriment. Warren told me in 1979 that no such cruel prank was ever inflicted
upon him or on anybody else. "Guthrie," he says, "had at least
that much civilization in town." His vehemence is good evidence of his sincerity. "That's a lie," he says. "That's a lie.
That's a bare-faced lie." But where could the lie, the mistake,
the forgetfulness, or the invention of such a story derive from?
Warren says "from evil, from enmity, from pride, from envy.
This time somebody would have been dead." This story follows
the persistent pattern of the others. Both sides agree that there
was harassment and unfair play, but they cannot agree on what
it was.

Warren remembers "a kind of difference, too, between the
railroad gang, the railroad town, and the brotherhood that
stayed on in that neighborhood, that gang, that was so God-
damn tough and the farm boys around who lived on the farms
around who could be tough but it was a different kind of
toughness, you see. And there was a lot of friction between
these two groups. Most of my friends were the country boys.
Sometimes really bloodletting fights broke out between town
and country boys. The country boys could take care of themselves." As a town boy allied with the rural boys, Warren
followed a difficult route. "The facts are that some of the persecutions are true. In general. But only one of these episodes you
have in mind," he told me, "ever happened."[95]

Many of the people of Guthrie tell similar stories, whether
they are true or false, for whatever motive. Very likely, the
tellings and the retellings accumulate exaggerated details, and
the likenesses of the stories derive from repetition instead of
sources and truth. Perhaps as the gossips add to their stories,
Warren also forgets, but he says, "I don't forget much." Just to
put the tales on paper results in what Warren calls an "over-
emphasis on the 'persecution' business."[95] Guthrie would not
be a provincial town if it did not talk—and in over sixty years
talk loses some of its truth and gains a good bit of error. But if
the town can talk, the poet can talk back. After I had told these
stories to Warren—many of them never told to him before—
and heard his answers and written an early draft of this chapter,

he had his say, so to speak, to the town: Many of the stories are total lies; many are exaggerations; many contain an element of truth.

One old acquaintance calls Warren a snob. "Maybe I was a snob," Warren comments. "I didn't seek the society of fools." Some who persecuted and who laughed at the persecutions say that Warren had a hard time because he was bright, that he was "always good natured," and that he was "easy to get along with," that he minded his own business, but that sometimes he would fight back.[58] From all the contradictions one consistency emerges. Warren was lonely. He has said that despite his love of the outdoors, the games, and some friends, he was "pretty lonely. Not lonesome, I wasn't lonesome, but I was alone a lot. I saw Guthrie as a place to be 'from.' "[54]

The Family

The family of Robert Penn Warren were not old-timers in Guthrie, but the families with whom they were friends in Warren's childhood were the old established farmers. The Warrens went out for weekends, or visitors came to visit them for dinner in town. Warren says he belonged to "a very closed family, and after the old farm families got old or died off nobody I can recollect (except an old bachelor friend of my father) ever came even to dinner. My father had one business friend, a partner in the bank, and he did dine very occasionally with them."

Warren says that the marriage of his parents, "was as perfect as possible. [My father] and my mother never once even raised their voices to each other, and somehow were always together, often hand in hand, in some deep private conversation. And they showed each other little considerations all the time. Yet they somehow managed to make the children feel totally included."[95]

One trait that held the mother and father together (and perhaps also Robert Penn and the second child, Mary) was literary, intellectual, and educational aspirations. The father as a young man had aspired to learning and to literary creation. Ruth Penn Warren, a teacher before her marriage, had many of the same desires; Mary Mexico Penn, sister of Ruth, taught school for years. With the help of her brother at Vanderbilt, Mary Warren even reviewed some books in the *Nashville Banner* on Donald Davidson's famous review page.* Warren wrote Davidson that "Sister is very anxious to do some reviewing and I took the liberty of letting her make a shot at the novel by Bodenheim. . . . If her review isn't satisfactory with you frankly let me know and I shall write one immediately. . . . If her work is all right she would be delighted to try her hand at something else, especially novels, for she is greatly interested in fiction."[86]

Mary was "really brilliant," Robert Penn says, but her father "unwittingly and in ignorance" had done her a wrong. He sent her to a small junior college (Warren calls it "a rotten school") and then to a little university (Kentucky Wesleyan) because he wanted to keep her from the world and to have her near at hand. (Though Vanderbilt was nearer—it was bigger.) In his later years the father said that he had not been given the right "situation of her intelligence." "She became a teacher in Maysville, Kentucky, married, had one daughter, and became some years ago a sort of local institution in that she had taught thousands of children—high school—in Maysville. In Maysville, she was, apparently, very sociable—at least with a circle of friends, mostly bridge players—bridge her passion. She used to visit Thomas, but finally ceased, I don't know why. . . . She had written 'novel' after 'novel,' even in grade school, and circulated the 'tablets' among a lot of people, to their great satisfaction. . . . I have always had the sneaking suspicion that she resisted writing or ever trying her hand seriously at it, because I was a writer—or wanted to be."[95] Mary and her father were close, but she and her older brother quarreled often, as he says, "aimlessly."

Warren's brother, Thomas, he believes, escaped some of the troubles of the older son. Six years younger than Robert Penn, he "came along as family troubles developed, and he did not get the same attention my sister and I had. Also he was a big burly

*An unsigned review of Maxwell Bodenheim's *Georgie May* appeared on page 7 of the magazine section of the *Tennessean* on 22 July 1928, about a month after Warren wrote Davidson as quoted here.

lad, and had seen me 'pushed around' some. Well, he wasn't to be pushed around. He was taught. His whole life may have been changed here."

Young Thomas cared less for education and the arts than Robert and Mary did. After a year or so he dropped out of the University of Kentucky. In the early Depression, at the time of his father's bankruptcy, he did various jobs, beginning as a laborer (on his first day of work he wore out a pair of gloves that cost more than he earned), became the operator of a grain elevator, and retired as a wealthy man. Thomas, Robert Penn says, has probably never read any of his author-brother's poetry or books. The young brother was nine when Robert Penn left home, but later, when they grew up, the two bothers developed a close relationship. "Now and then we took hunting trips to North Carolina together for days." They sit together and talk, Robert Penn says, but not in words.

Robert Penn Warren was generally an obedient son, although he did not have what he calls "a lot of 'don'ts and do's.' You did your work, but your free time was your own. I wandered where I would." Thomas was a different breed, less bookish, more independent. Once when the older son came home for the summer from Vanderbilt, Thomas led a gathering that caused some tiptoeing around Mrs. Warren and the household for a few days. Robert wrote that

Matters here are in such an unstable condition now that obedience is certainly a policy of rare discretion. The waters are troubled as a consequence of Thomas' recent fiasco in the nature of an alcoholic brawl. It appears that he procured two bottles of aged and potent wine and seduced the youth of the town into an all night session in a tent which he and another child here have erected. He has been accustomed to sleep out in it, so his absence was not alarming that night. The next morning the town was electrified by the news. The little Frey boy became disturbed about the probable consequences and turned state's evidence to save his own hide. The matter is especially disgraceful since a Methodist revival is now in full swing. Good God![89]

Thomas's early encounter with alcohol in this fashion was a violation of the drinking customs in the Warren household. "When we were children," Warren says, father never drank. But when I was in college, on a visit home, I was studying one evening while my father was reading. I opened my suit-case, took out a bottle of bourbon, got ice, and poured myself a drink. (There had *never* been any *lecturing* on the subject.) In the calmest voice imaginable, my father said: "Won't you offer me one?" So I fixed him one and we drank together. As always thereafter with female blessing. Father once told me that he "drank as young men do," but as a father did not want to set young boys a bad example. One should be "adult" to drink. He said that he did not "feel right" about "setting an exam-ple" of law-breaking for the young during Prohibition. Very character-istic. On visits to my house he always drank—moderately. And wine, moderately.[95]

Warren's father through all the years was probably the most significant influence on the poet's thinking. Strength of charac-ter, wisdom, common sense were the things the son always recalled: "A few odds and ends about my father hit me," War-ren wrote in 1979.

About race, long before the stir started he once remarked to me: "I've always found that if you treat any man decently, black or white, he'll probably treat you the same way." Another, off-hand remark: "One of the most important things you have to learn in life is to deny yourself." This in relation, I think, to his taking on the family burden after the death of his father and his older brother's flight to Mexico. I don't think I've mentioned to you that he, though very unchurch, sent us to Sunday School as a way of studying the Bible. He paid me to read it the first time (three chapters a day for a year will do it with a few extras left over—I seem to remember). The first time I read it he paid me. Then I read it twice on my own by the time of college. But I hated to go (didn't have to go) to church. I tried to talk myself in-to some religion in my freshman year at college, but no dice/ Vice won. But I kept on reading the Old Testament. This last winter one of the things I read Eleanor (with commentaries) was the New Testa-ment.[95]

As Warren remembered his father, he was a man of contra-dictions, love and reserve, strength and gentleness, silence and striking, sudden, conclusive remarks, determination or ambi-tion and acceptance:

Only once I ever heard him swear. He was a very gentle and uncritical man, but capable of quick decisive action. He wouldn't have a firearm in the house (to my great anguish) but he kept a revolver in his desk at the bank (I get [gather?] it was rusted). But when a prowler woke him up one night, he seized an iron poker and damned near killed him, blood everywhere, the victim finally diving throught the glass window of a bathroom. My father said quite calmly: If I had had on some footwear I would have pursued him. (There was snow on the ground and blood for a hundred yards or so next morning.) My father was ill once in his life. Never a day in bed until forty (when he had a gall bladder operation, typhoid fever, and pneumonia, without even getting out of bed—a nightmare, that period, the swish of the skirts and the rubbery sound of the shoes of the trained nurse). Then he didn't spend another day in bed until he had to prop up a leg for a day when he was 83. His death was peculiar. He fell on the floor one day unconscious. The doctor found that he was in the last stages of cancer of the prostate. My father had never mentioned it to anyone, and had never seen a doctor, never went to a dentist in his life, though in old age he remarked: "I must confess that lately I've removed a couple myself." Not a Christian Scientist. Just iron willed. If my mother's toe ached he'd have two doctors in. When he was 83, he and I took a long trip together to Mexico and Cuba, and he damned near killed me with his energy. We did a lot of wandering around America together to "see the country." And he wanted to talk about the books he had been reading. He was courteous to all, but had no friends in the latter part of his life. His friends had been of an older generation, and he had no interest in common with the people around him. Except his love for his grandchildren, and his work with Thomas. Thomas couldn't swing things without him. But it was a lonely life.

I guess I had forgotten to mention that his plans (hopes) had been to be a lawyer and writer. I'd find Blackstone and things like that stuck away. I thought he had finally destroyed them.[95]

Opinions of Robert Franklin Warren cover a wide range. Some believed he had no force or personality; many admired him; some called him "the finest man" they knew. He was engaged in many financial enterprises, sometimes successful, but he also had a period of failure, "severe financial reverses, due to the failure of a man who owed him a relatively large amount."[91] At great cost to himself as a young man he had helped to raise his father's children. Robert Penn says, "He broke his back at it, but he said, 'It was too late for me. . . . I couldn't do everything.'" But it was too late only for his highest aspirations. Late in his life he said, "I've had a very happy life, and I've tried to fulfill my obligations and do my duty."[122] He even said that he took "joy in my obligations."[43]

Robert Penn Warren did not like to visit his step-grandmother, but he went obediently at the command of his father. Virginia or Jenny Warren did not share the boy's interest in history, talk, stories, and poetry. Each year he had to spend one weekend, one day and night, with his paternal step-grandmother. "That was always an agony to me, because they had none of the same interests and conversation, you see."[53] "She is a good woman," Robert Franklin told his son, "and she has done the best she could. Because you find her dull and stupid is no reason why you shouldn't spend a day there as a matter of decency, you see."[25] "It was," Warren says, "a torture of dullness," but he visited. He prowled around the attic, looking at old books bought by his father and grandfather. He served out the time of the required visit. Even the deceased grandfather, Warren concluded, had been "a very crotchety man in many ways. I know nothing about him, my Father told me only one fact about him. For instance, he said, 'Oh, he was in the Civil War,—Shiloh and other battles . . .' (as was his brother at Shiloh, and Grandpa Penn). Father wouldn't go on with the subject."[95]

Robert Franklin Warren's last days were lonely. "He was totally alone in the last part of his life," his son says, "and I've never understood this isolation that he imposed on himself. One thing about it, I think nobody around was interested in the things he was interested in. Nobody around with the same interests. So he would just rather read than talk about things that didn't interest him." This was the culmination of a lifetime of reading. When years later his son wrote a long essay on Cooper, he read the same texts that his father had read years before him. "I noticed at the end of every novel there was the date when he had finished it—1891 or whatever it was. He was very methodical. Later, he was reading Freud, Marx, and things like that as well as poetry and history."[43]

Even in his old age, the father remembered his early efforts at poetry, and he even lost some of his shyness. When Warren was about fifty, his father, now "an old, old man, way up in his eighties" mailed his son "a poem or two he had found in his papers—on old yellow paper falling apart, and the old purple type ribbon that he had used back in the nineties—without comment; he just sent those to me in an envelope. By this time the father was aware that the son had "carried on what he had wanted to do."[95] After Robert Franklin Warren's death, Warren recently learned, Mary Warren found the book with his poems in it.

Robert Penn Warren says that he himself is not a believer, but that he is a great "yearner." The Warrens were very "unchurchy. They were good citizens . . . but unchurchy. My father wasn't even a member of a church until very late in life, and that was just church as a worthy social institution. My father was in a way an old-fashioned, you know, freethinker. Put it this way, he was of a religious temperament and a man of the most ferocious honesty and ferocious sense of obligation. . . . And great kindness to people, great kindness."[54] Again, his son said, "My father didn't demand love. But he sure commanded respect. He was a very gentle man except when confronted by a lie."[95]

Considering the characters of the father and the son, it is not amazing that one of the first topics to jump into the mind as one ponders Warren's novels is the subject of the relationship—or kinds of relationships—between fathers and sons. His novels treat the alienated father and son, the son returning to the father, the search (thwarted or not) for a father, the love of the two (sometimes the love of one for the other without the other knowing it), the son's hostility to his father and his heritage, the son's carrying out or rebelling against the most holy aims of the father, and so on and on. In the poetry perhaps not even the love of man and woman is much more frequent or exalted subject than the many kinds of relationships of fathers and sons. Shortly after 1955 Katherine Anne Porter wrote a most touching letter to her friend Robert Penn Warren after she heard of the events at the time of his father's death:

The thought of your father suffering by himself because he didn't want to be trouble to any one is very painful; and must be to you. It was very heroic and characteristic, maybe he did what he wished to do, it takes very pure courage, surely above all at that age, to know death is near, and not ask any one to know what is happening. It is customary to say, one is born and dies alone. Not true about birth at least, which mother and child must certainly share, and not just in the body. Death is a solitary thing, yet the living *should* take their part in love and help, there is a sharing and how happy you must be to have been told even at so late an hour, and to have been with your father to say good bye to him. I love his toughness of spirit, but he shouldn't have expected you to be tough about him! But then, I remember the wonderful passage in *Brother to Dragons* (Red, I keep thinking of that title as *Blood of Dragons*) when in his fathers [sic] company the poet had begun to understand the nature of happiness—I am sure everything was clear and right in his mind, but I understand the nature of loneliness—xxxx.[87]

Warren did not write so much about his mother as his father. One reason may be that she died in 1931, when Warren was only twenty-six, and twenty to twenty-five years before he began to write lyric poetry about family characters. Years later as he wrote, he knew the presence of his father as well as the memory. But there are several strong and loving mothers in Warren's fiction. One of the strongest is the iron-willed mother of the protagonist in *A Place to Come To.* Lucy Stark in *All the King's Men* fails to make a man of her son only because of the flaws of her demagogic husband.

When Ruth Warren appears directly in a poem or when she is a prototype of a character, she always is depicted with love and admiration.

Ruth Penn Warren was woman in her own right. "In my entire life," Warren says, "she never belonged to any club. She never referred to having been to club meetings of some sort before my birth."[95] She was not "overly active in the church," as one friend put it.[69] If she was not the head of the household, she was certainly the head of the children, and most especially the head of Robert Penn Warren. She was able to give Warren freedom to commute by train to Clarksville High School twelve miles away when he was only fifteen, but she kept control when his health was not very good. After Warren went to Vanderbilt, he once wrote Allen Tate, "Auditory stimulations from the inner shrine convey the general import that I am to go to bed and that right quickly."[89] One school teacher who knew Mrs. Warren well says that "nobody disliked her intensely," but that she was not by any means the most popular woman in town. And Warren says that she had no desire to be. She "choked her younguns" down peoples' throats, the teacher says, and they made fun of her because she was so close, so stingy, and so careful with her money. A loving and proud mother can be irritating. From her son's perspective, "she was always very courteous, but held a distance. A couple of women made 'calls' about every two weeks in the afternoon—a Mrs. Susan Downer, I remember, is one. But these lived in the country. Mother had no real 'friend' in town. And never gossiped."

When Warren left for college, his mother said, "Whatever you do, just don't tell me anything about it."[95] But even after Warren had completed his first degree at Vanderbilt and worked most of a year on his second at California, his mother was capable of taking a strong hand in his affairs. Yale offered Warren a scholarship while he was working on a degree at the University of California, and Warren "unfortunately transmitted . . . to my mother" the possibility that he would take French leave from the University of California. The troubled mother, as Warren said, "wrote to the President's office here to ask them if a more regular mode of leave-taking were possible. The President's office replied in great wrath that the guy who pulled out as I had intended would be guilty of a grievous offence and could expect no further good will from this dump."[90] Warren's mother was an excellent host to his friends from Vanderbilt, a courteous lady of the house, a woman of manners, but other traits could create, as in this instance, great difficulties—even when she was right and Warren was about to make a fool of himself. After all, at some stage a man does have the right to decide when to be his own fool.

Like almost all families of moderate means in the South, the Warrens customarily had a black servant in the household,

whose relationship with the family was often close. Warren
wrote one poem (discussed in a later chapter) about the death
of a woman who worked for his family, Seeley (Cecilia) Brad-
shaw. He describes her as a "second 'mother,' friend, tale
teller."[95] When she married and left the Warrens, she named her
first son for Robert Penn. Geraldine Carr and Savannah (it was
a custom of Southerners black and white to name girls after
cities and states) also were employed by the Warrens at different times and for long periods, as he remembers. Kent Greenfield said Savannah worked for Mrs. Warren a long time.
Decades after Mrs. Warren died, Kent said, Savannah remembered that she liked Mrs. Warren more than any employer she
ever had.[72] One of the nurses or maids, a mulatto, even taught
the children to read and write, according to one acquaintance.[73]
Another story—a more likely one—is that young Robert Penn
read Tarzan novels to Savannah.

Until recently it has not been widely known that Warren is
blind in one eye, yet the accident was perhaps the most momentous event is his younger years. I first asked Warren's brother
about the blindness. We had agreed that when I asked a question in an interview and he did not wish to discuss it he would
just say, "Let's not talk about that." So Thomas said, "Let's not
talk about that." Lester Lannom also told an interviewer in an
oral history project that he simply did not wish to talk about
it.

Thomas threw a rock and accidentally hit Robert Penn in the
eye. Some in the community say Warren was lying in the yard
and Thomas was across a hedge or some bushes from him.
Playfully, Thomas threw a rock or two over the hedge, not
knowing his brother was there. One of the rocks hit Warren
directly in the eye. As Warren remembers the accident, he says,
"I have no recollection whatever except this one stone-a piece
of cinder coming out of the air when I was lying on my back
with my hands under my head." "I was lying there in the
evening. And I was lying down looking up at the sky just
looking up at the evening sky, and he was on the other side and
picked up a piece of cinder, I guess it was, and aimlessly tossed

it over the hedge. He didn't know I was there. It was purely accidental. It happened to fall in my eye."

Some say that for many years there was a deep hostility and anger between Thomas and Red because of the accident. Warren calls the story of the estrangement "all a big lie. . . . This is really a big lie. I felt so sorry for Thomas because he suffered so. That's another aspect of it," he told me. "It made us closer," he says. "In fact, even now I am almost tearful." Again his story differs from the tales of the town. Thomas threw only one rock, not several, according to his brother, and the first one fatefully hit Warren precisely in the eye and blinded him. "Who else was present?" Warren asks and then answers himself: "Nobody!" Psychologically, it seems to me, Warren's statement—that he felt sympathy for the accidental injurer—is much more believable than the reports of those Warren calls "ignorant guessers" outside the family.[95]

The physical results were immediate, and the effects on Warren's plans for a lifetime career came abruptly. He had been admitted to Annapolis; now he could not go. But the long-term consequences were more significant. Not until the late 1970s could Warren speak with anyone about the eye or even think about it, and even then not without some agitation. His talk now is evidence of extreme and developing psychological effects:

I felt sort of alienated rather than emasculated, but alienated. That would be the word I usually would use to myself. Alienation and separation from other people, and I felt a kind of shame—shame is not the word—but disqualification for life, as if I had lost a leg, say, or an arm or something. That or some sense of being maimed, you see. . . . It made you feel unattractive, and it made you also express your anger quite a lot. Or hoard it quite a lot. I mean it made you get much more ready to blow at somebody.[95]

He feared further physical consequences. When he arrived at college, he "learned that if eyesight gets to going in one eye, it may go in both, a sympathetic effect. So I began to have nightmares, and the waiting worriment about going blind in the other eye." Warren denies that a thwarted love affair was the cause of his attempted suicide at Vanderbilt. But the psychological consequences of the loss of his eye and perhaps a temporary despair over his accomplishments in writing may have been contributory. But the effects were deeper, at least for the literary world, even than despair and attempted suicide. In ways that will probably never be known, the injury governed the writing and the subject matter of his poetry. A particular despair may lead to a kind of psychological or philosophical depression—or to accomplishment. The injury, Warren says, "was the source of many of the poems, or appeared in many of the poems in disguised form."[95]

The early poems are usually so universalized or abstracted in subject matter or event that probably neither Warren's memory nor an expert psychiatrist could fathom those connections. But it may be possible to see the old injury even in the particular poems about events Warren had known in Cerulean and Guthrie. It can lurk in the feelings of evil in "Dragon Country," in the story of the mass family murder of the Gillum children, in the story of the death of a boy who fell between moving boxcars, in the story of the introverted albino cobbler (Mr. Moody), in the threats of the mad druggist to fill prescriptions with poison, and so on. But the end of this topic is speculation, for no one, not even the poet, can ever fully and exactly extract the connections between the eye injury and other evils of his childhood days and the poetry.

After Warren's days at Vanderbilt and California the ties between him and Guthrie began to diminish, and they lessened more with the death of the mother in 1931. He had a close friendship with the outdoorsman, the drunken failed baseball pitcher who returned to the outdoors—Kent Greenfield—but he felt few attachments to the old things he had known in Guthrie. He married Cinina Brescia in September 1930. Mrs. Warren died about a year later. Several times he brought Cinina to Guthrie, and for years he visited his father when there were good opportunities, sometimes too far apart. On a few occasions—very few—he brought his second wife, Eleanor Clark, and his two children to Guthrie. His second wife and his father, Warren says, "were 'close' in a strange way, all the years." But Warren probably has made more trips to Kentucky for research on his works than he has to the town of Guthrie.

Living in his homes in Connecticut and Vermont, Warren contends that he has as close a relationship to the old South he had known as he would have if he had returned to Guthrie— an "abstract" community. The present citizens of Guthrie, except for those who knew him of old, seem almost totally unaware of Warren as a man or poet. His best friend, Kent Greenfield, said in the last year he lived that Guthrie has never sufficiently recognized Warren. "If I was Robert Penn," Kent said, "I'd never put my foot in this town again as long as I lived. They should have put something up in his memory, wudn't nothing but a little old plaque. Darndest place I ever saw in my life."[62] And well also they might "put something up" for Kent, but the old sportsman was not a man to think in terms of himself.

One has to select the people he questions if he is to find anyone who has ever heard of Robert Penn Warren or *All the King's Men,* book or movie, in Guthrie. The county newspaper ran only one story about Warren between the time of his maturity and the summer of 1976.* As the Warrens leave Guthrie, so do the memories of them. Thomas has three daughters. Like their Aunt Mary and Uncle Robert, two of them have fled Guthrie and in 1977 one of the two died of an aneurism in flight back to France, where she lived. One daughter remains in Guthrie, Mrs. R.D. Frey. A conversation with her revealed the most complete and pleasant portrait of Robert Penn Warren among his relatives that I have heard. She knows "Uncle Robert Penn" as an uncle more than as a literary figure. She is not able to read his poetry (a remark heard over and over, probably

---

*One man said that I did not find people who knew Warren during that summer simply because I did not search enough, because I did not see the right ones. The next summer he provided me with a list of a half dozen I had failed to see. Not one person whose name he gave me knew Warren well and was available for an interview. During the two summers I tried for nearly three weeks to see one old citizen of Guthrie, but he was never available and willing.

because most laymen maintain that they cannot read any poetry). She read *All the King's Men* in the summer of 1976 and
enjoyed it thoroughly. She believes that the cemetery in *Band
of Angels* is the cemetery in Guthrie. She did not like *Wilderness*
because she found that it was too depressing. She has not been
offended or annoyed by the language or the morals of Warren's
books as so many of her acquaintances have. She remembers
well with love her Grandfather Robert Franklin Warren, who
died when she was between thirteen and fifteen, but he was
very old when she knew him. On television, she says, her uncle
looked exactly like his father, her grandfather.

For a long time Robert Penn came to Guthrie at least once a
year and stayed with Mrs. Frey's father, Thomas. As far as she
knows, he liked Guthrie. She believes that the town has ignored
her famous literary uncle. At the sesquicentennial celebration
several years ago, Robert Penn Warren's name was not even
mentioned as one of the famous natives of the town. On one
trip her uncle asked her what she wanted for Christmas, and
later he sent her the Girl Scout watch she asked for. That was
about 1949 or 1950, before Warren had any children of his own.
When he came, he played with her, talked to her, spent time
with her. The author and the little girl played taxicab, and he
would graciously pay her twenty-five cents for his imaginary
ride. As she became a little older Uncle Robert reached a point
where he did not play taxi much any more, and they played
cards, a three- or four-handed game of Dirty Eight or Crazy
Eight. Later, in her teens, she really wanted, she later told her
uncle, a sports Buick with real leopard-skin seats. Warren says,
"But she didn't think I could afford it. Right, she was."

The Boy and the Poetry

The general and extensive discrepancies between Robert Penn
Warren's memories of his harassments in his childhood and the
stories of his community are perhaps not unusual. It is not
beyond the realm of possibility that some such stories spring
altogether from the cruelty of some minds, that the tales derive
not from boyhood cruelty but from the inhumanity of haters
of men or haters of this man or of success.

In this chapter I have let the community have its say, and Warren has sometimes disagreed and objected to what was said, but he has not asked me to delete anything uncomplimentary to himself. He has requested a change here and there when the comment might touch a sore or tender spot that would hurt someone else.

Person to person, Warren is a man of extraordinary kindness, good manners, considerateness, good cheer, and helpfulness even to those who may never be able to return the help. Though friendly, he protects himself vigorously. He withdraws from all contact with the world for hours nearly every day and then returns to the family and the ordinary world for another part of the day. He procrastinates in writing letters, and he is forgetful, but he is extraordinarily kind when he finally gets around to replying to the strangers who are critics or scholars studying his works. With the Fugitives and the Agrarians, he has been independent, firm, at times even adamant in his opinions. He defends his positions with humor, reasoned argument, rhetoric, and occasional heat. But his vehemence does not extend to animosity or pettiness or bullying. He is open in his emotional responses. He was capable of heated argument with, say, Davidson or Tate before their deaths, but he would openly weep or shake uncontrollably with grief after he had seen such a close friend on his deathbed. The harassments of Guthrie may have had extraordinary effects on Warren; they may have affected his writing about violence and his view that man is not perfect or perfectible or even moving toward perfectibility. But the adversities of childhood have not, so far as I can tell, or so far as I have ever heard anyone say, had any effect on Warren's psyche. The small boy became a big and firm and loving and gentle man, kind to others, confident of himself.

These have been many of the details of which Robert Penn Warren's poetry has been made. From this time, these places, and these people have emerged the best he has written. This is the context, though I would not like to be so fancy as to call it the contextual basis, for his poetic art. This chapter contains much biography, but it is not a biography. There has not been enough examination of the poems themselves even to call it what Brooks and Warren regard as reductive criticism. Let it simply be a sketch, without even the conventions that might have been attached to that term in the days of the old-fashioned sketches of Irving and Hawthorne.

Whatever it is, it is fundamental to Warren. There are no direct connections between some of this sketch and his later poetry; for some poems perhaps there are hardly any indirect connections. The poet springs from the man, the man from the boy, and the boy from his community and his heritage. Warren has continued to write distinguished poetry at an age when most poets have begun writing poor verse or quit altogether or gone to some reward besides a Pulitzer Prize. More than most, he has turned backward and backward to the facts and the spirit of his past when he lived in Guthrie and visited in Cerulean Springs before he went to Vanderbilt. There are poems unquestionably and obviously set in Kentucky, New England, the West, and Italy, but there are few set directly in the times and places of the days between Guthrie and Warren's second marriage. In the fiction, yes, but the poetry, no. Or at least not much —a poem or so about Louisiana perhaps, but not many.

Several times Warren has suggested that the writer finds many of his materials in his childhood and his early years. "You carry some place with you in your head. For example, even a lot of those late poems are really autobiographical—things that really happened." Many had "germs" in something that happened long before. The subjectivity and the feelings of the heart make the poetry since 1950 personal and factual at the same time. "It's much more inside; you're reliving your life. For me, anyway." Warren does not deliberately make a poem factual; for the sake of the poetry he makes changes. The consequences are better poetry and errors in biography when part truths are taken for whole truths.[95] The old things nearly always get into the poem in some way, sometimes recognizable, sometimes not. The past helps to create the mood of the poem and of life. The child's life and the marriage and happy fatherhood seem to govern the tone of the poem. The mystery of poetry and of its background is that things can be felt but are difficult to name.

"I've been modified by a thousand things in places I've lived, but I can't conceive of writing a novel, say, which didn't have its southern reference. . . . You can't change such things; they're part of you."[46] All the novels have had a direct "southern reference," but only a few have had a context identifiably based on Warren's childhood. Far more than the fiction, many of the poems have had a personal, an autobiographical, a Todd County or Trigg County reference. Both Warren and his wife, Eleanor Clark, have a firm sense of place. Asked whether they "see connections among place, self and society that those in an a-communal context may miss," Warren replies: "That's based on a quest for an old-fashioned American community and a sense of firmly fixed family. By firmly fixed, I mean families that are real families. That makes a vast difference." And Eleanor Clark adds: "Also we both came from families with an extraordinarily perceptive sense of the American past. His grandfathers and my grandfathers—for all their great difference of place—had a similar sense of what the whole American experience was, and would talk about it in similar ways, as we have found out from each other over the years."[45]

Once Warren considered coming back South to live. Eleanor Clark suggested shortly after they married that they move to Tennessee for at least part of the year. She told him when they had children they "shouldn't deny them the kind of boyhood you had in your summers. They ought to see some of that."[55] But the country had now become a country of the memory and of the mind. The place and the people Warren had known were gone. It was no longer a place to come to. Even the rural South had become a country of mechanized farms, often of thousands of acres. So Connecticut became the home of the Warrens in the winter. They lived in Europe a great deal, with children in foreign schools, traveled a bit. He taught one term a year at Yale, lived not a great distance from New York (though still refusing to have television in his home), and wrote. He has an unlisted telephone number, gives out the number to only a few people, and asks them to call him only at certain hours of the day. Partly he retires to write; partly he cuts himself off from whatever local community there may be about him. The place of his childhood exists only in memory and in his works.

Culturally and geographically, Warren's country of the past and of the mind no longer has a physical reality. When he ceases writing, his country will vanish. In the meantime, perhaps with a few exceptions, his works still have the same basic contexts that he knew at the beginning of his career. Warren says that his late poetry is based on actuality, and usually that actuality was related to his childhood.

You do always write about your childhood—if ever you had one to write about. Allen Tate told me that Warren and many Southern writers had to leave the South because the South ran them out (Tate had particularly in mind Warren's leaving LSU when that institution did not meet an offer from the University of Minnesota) and because the South as the writer knew it in his early life no longer exists. There is exile from an author's native region, but it is accompanied by alienation only part of the time. Peter Stitt recently asked Warren whether he still regarded himself as a Southern writer despite his long absence. Warren replied, "I can't be anything else. You are what you are. I was born and grew up in Kentucky, and I think your early images survive. Images mean a lot of things besides pictures."[42]

·3·

Guthrie & Cerulean Springs

MANY AMERICAN writers in the twentieth century have created imaginary regions or towns, and in some of them families, characters, and bits of stories appear and reappear in separate works. Some of the literary places have passed through historical stages and processes resembling the actual development of American communities—the establishment of settlements on the frontier and their gradual maturing into towns. Most major American writers, perhaps especially those from the South, have spent their childhoods in small communities and have written about them during most of their creative years. Only in the latter part of the twentieth century have writers come from urban areas in significant numbers. Even Dreiser, itinerant citizen of Chicago and New York, remained an Indiana boy who had moved to the city.

Some fictional places have become famous because of their existence in a single work. The most notable American town created in one novel, perhaps, is Sinclair Lewis's Gopher Prairie. One kind of American literary accomplishment has been the creation of an identifiable place in a number of related works. The most extensive and well known, of course, is Jefferson in Faulkner's Yoknapatawpha County. Others are Robinson's Tilbury Town, Frost's country north of Boston, Masters's Spoon River, Anderson's Winesburg, Hemingway's upper Michigan and Nick Adams country (interrelated, but never put together by Hemingway himself), Welty's town in the stories of *The Golden Apples,* Wolfe's Altamont and Libya Hill, and perhaps another dozen or a score of works related to each other and centered on one place. Mark Twain's Hannibal and Willa Cather's Red Cloud each appear in more than one book, but under different names. In some of her Southern stories, Katherine Anne Porter created a family moving westward, carrying along even the graveyard, or the remains of the corpses, as they move from state to state before settling permanently in Texas.

Robert Penn Warren's novels cover a vast range of space and time, mostly in Southern history, and they have no common setting. His collected poems, however, do contain, surprisingly, materials that seem to assemble themselves into a created town, a place that also appears in several of the short stories and in *Night Rider.* The locale is generally consistent in a number of poems about the boy and his family. A childhood friend (in the short story "Luke Goodwood Comes Back" and "American Portrait: Old Style"), plays a substantial role. One lynching is used as the basis for particular details in the early poem "Pondy Woods" and also in the later "Ballad of Mister Dutcher and the last Lynching in Gupton." In all, there are about forty poems that develop characters and narrative situations, fill out the population, and create the life of Warren's poetic town. These are in addition to a good number of poems about Warren's own childhood family.

Warren himself has not publicly acknowledged the existence of such a town in his works. "As memory offered suggestions," he says, with no conscious plan, he has written about his youth and his home town.[95] He has pointed out incidents, images, and even entire poems taken from realities he knew in his childhood. The sources are mainly derived from Guthrie, Kentucky, where Warren spent the brief years before he went for a year to the high school at nearby Clarksville, Tennessee. Some of the poems ultimately come from Cerulean, Kentucky, where both his parents grew up, and where he spent summers with his grandfather from the age of six to thirteen. But the poetic town also derives from other actual places. "Boy Wandering in Simms' Valley" is drawn from a lonely rural area in Vermont, but it seems to be moved into the South, transsubstantiated in some fashion to fit the real country of Warren's childhood and the poetic town of his works. "Dragon Country: To Jacob Boehme" is a collection from diverse sources of particular images to recreate a Southern myth heard in almost every community, though it does name Warren's native county, Todd, and the local Pinch 'Em Church.

Creation of a town in American literature has a distinct effect on the form and the content, even the technique, of the separate parts of the chronicle. One who knows a community is acquainted with a goodly number of people who associate with each other frequently, who have individualistic and eccentric ways well known to their neighbors, some of whom live a constant and unchanging life, and some whom suddenly and perhaps tragically shift from their previous constancy. The literary career of a town often relies on some variation of the form of a character sketch. The author may see the character in a long historical tradition that the subject-character himself or herself has never thought about or perhaps even heard of. The author creates a series of vignettes of events or portraits in a single work (like the section on Altamont waking in *Look Homeward, Angel*), or he develops stories and characters and monologues in a series of works, as in Frost's narrative and dramatic poems about the country people of New England. Despite a wide diversity of people, the community itself seems to develop a culture and identity that represents both the variety of its citizens and the thematic, philosophical, and religious interests of its literary creator. The poetic community has its own population, but some of the people are brought from foreign places and given native ways.

The complexity of Warren's town derives from several places he has known, and its diversities create considerable difficulty in organizing any discussion of it. In the poems that do or could belong to this country of Warren's mind there is a wide variety of time settings (a historical span from the 1920s to the 1970s), of characters, of actions, of play and occupations, of attitudes, race, religion—indeed, a wide variety of all the many things it takes to make a town.

Theme, person, setting, and image in each work assume an identity separate from all the actual sources or prototypes. The poet has described the origins of several poems; and local citizens remember or think they remember people and events resembling those in many of the other poems.

The techniques Warren used in creating his community vary greatly from piece to piece. There are almost pure narratives, short narratives that end with long poetic fables, reminiscences, character sketches, meditations that contain a little narration, and a variety of other genres. Multifarious as the methods and subjects and characters are, they add up to some kind of place. Although one of the poems may be derived from several aspects of Warren's experiences and his imagination, it could not be transported harmoniously into another's works. It would be a stranger in another writer's land. The heart of Warren's town —as in other imagined towns—is probably identifiable mainly by the heart of the creator, but that fact does not destroy the image of a community. Indeed, the close association between an author and a particular place (real and imagined) is an unusual aspect of a national literature in itself so broad that it has but little homogeneity.

Warren's return to his childhood came in distinct stages. From the time when he became a Fugitive at Vanderbilt until the poems of the early fifties he used poetic subjects from Guthrie only vaguely and occasionally. In the 1920s and 1930s he did write and discard, he says, "a certain number of 'local' poems." Although he has said that many of his poems have derived indirectly and in disguise from his blindness in one eye, autobiographical origins in the early poems are usually not discernible. "Terror" (1941), however, has one veiled allusion to Warren's youth. Warren says it refers to Harry Lyle, a friend and classmate at Clarksville, who "crashed a private plane a few years after he had become a pharmacist—or at least worked in a drug store—in an air crash as he was learning to fly, not the war."[95] In the late 1920s he wrote about a lynching and a lovers' tryst on Vinegar Hill (the latter never republished), but he did not explicitly treat materials about his own life. Thirty years later, in *Promises* (1957), he returned to Guthrie and to particular people, events, and scenes in several poems, and for the first time he wrote about the personal life of his family—his wife and his two children. But still he did not write much about his sister and brother and his father and mother. (An exception to this pattern, just a few years before *Promises,* is the treatment in *Brother to Dragons* of the relationship with his father.) His mother is a central figure in "Country Burying (1919)" and "undeveloped references to family history" appear in "Lullaby: Moonlight Lingers" and in "Founding Fathers."[95]

Early Poems

Faint glimmers of Kentucky rural life appear as early as the issue of *The Fugitive* for December 1924, but the homeliness of the title, "Alf Burt, Tenant Farmer," points out sharply the unreality of the afterlife described in the poem. Except for his name, Alf is not much more like a true Southern farmer than one of Housman's plowboys. He has already departed from the hard life of a small Southern farm and gone to a vague place of oblivion or eternity where "No dream can fall to stir him to remember / Thistle and drouth and the crops that never came." Alf becomes a departed soul and remains a concept, not a person in a poem.

Six months later in *The Fugitive* of June 1925, Warren wrote of Southern life, this time of Nashville and an athletic event. "The Wrestling Match" is the first published poetry or prose by Warren that treats (even fragmentarily and briefly) dialect, character, and a crowd situation that are identifiably Southern enough to presage the flavor of the later regional fiction and poems. As a student at Vanderbilt Warren attended heavyweight wrestling matches of men like the fabulous Strangler Lewis. This may be the least traditional poem in all the issues of *The Fugitive,* the one most different from the sophisticated and often high-toned poetry of Tate and Ransom. The first stanza is the best:

> "Here in this corner, ladies and gentlemen,
> I now presents 'Mug' Hill, weight two-hundred-ten,

Who will wrestle here tonight the "Battling Pole,'
Boruff—" who, as insistently the stale

Loud voice behind asserts, is good as hell.

In *The Sewanee Review* for that same year Warren published
"August Revival: Crosby Junction," a poem filled with a rather
precise and unusual account of southern Kentucky rural life.
Country fundamentalist revivals had been written about more
by the old Southwest humorists than by the poets of Nashville,
and Warren linked the religious practice with a name for a
railroad town, a "junction," which might have been like Guthrie. The subject would remain with Warren for many years until
he wrote *World Enough and Time* and the poem "Amazing
Grace" (1977). Revivals in the South come at the farmers' lay-
ing-by time, when the "Wheat is threshed and cut the heavy
clover." Then there is time for religion.

The country church is somewhat sophisticated for most parts
of the rural South at the time. Warren writes of an "oaken organ
top," "red geranium petals," and "varnished benches." After
three stanzas describing the inside of the church and the congregation, Warren addresses the minister: "Enough—O you behind the pulpit there. . . . / Enough, old man! Eat, sleep, for you
are old, / And your chronicle [his sermon on salvation] too
weary to be told." The poem ends with images of a dead world
after the harvest and of a religion little more alive than the
earth. Possibly speaking of the Christ, Warren writes, "Touch
no more the broken feet, nor touch / The piteous brown fingers
in the shroud. / But let them so be. . . ." That is, apparently
there is no resurrection for the Christ such as the Crosby Junction congregation had hoped for.

Warren decided not to include "Vinegar Hill" (see below)
and "August Revival" in the volumes of his poetry, but for my
taste they are better than some of the poems he did retain.
"August Revival" especially anticipates some of the best of
Warren's writing about his great unsatisfied yearning for a belief in God that he never attained.

The backwoods and the country as a locale are treated extensively in a group of poems written in 1927, "Kentucky Moun-

tain Farm." Poetically, the collection has no identifiable personae, is not populated by men. As Faulkner might have seemed a little super-sophisticated—anything but local—in his early poems and in the second novel, *Mosquitoes,* Warren also did not at first reveal much about his own roots in the small town and the soil (Agrarian though he was). In most of the early poems Warren was much more traditionally poetic than local. There was a "romantic and distant detachment from [the] real self."[95] "Kentucky Mountain Farm" was more about the air and the rocks than it was about the tillage of the earth and the tillers. A few early stories were the first works truly to reveal the country in the writer, and the best of these suggest how, as Warren said many times later, a story might have been a poem if the poet had not turned away from what he later regarded as a better genre to write short fiction. The good local stories are "When the Light Gets Green" (1936), an account of how a child's grandfather had a stroke; "Christmas Gift" (1937), a superb early story of a childhood; "Goodwood Comes Back" (1941), in the early part a study in depth of childhood and a boy like Kent Greenfield; and "Blackberry Winter" (1946), often regarded as Warren's best piece of short fiction. Guthrie people would also have recognized the fidelity of the fiction to their world and their history in the first published novel, *Night Rider* (1939).

The seven lyrical parts of "Kentucky Mountain Farm," written when Warren was an immature as well as a young poet, were an early promise that he would later turn to his native earth as a subject. The manner and the images derive from some of the ways of the Fugitive group, from traditional and mannered poetry, more than from a farm, the mountains, and Todd County. Ultimately the subject springs from Southern mountains, which Warren says he had then never seen, but the poems also perhaps show the influence of the division in Todd County between the small hill farms in the north and the large rich bottomland farms in the south. But despite the setting, the poems are directed more to the great world than to the people of one particular region and community. Many of the images, of course, may be found in Kentucky and the hills east of Elkton

in Todd County, but they also may be found generally in much
of the South or almost anywhere else. Warren has written that
the poem "for me was a pure invention—I had never seen
Eastern Kentucky—and a little of East Tennessee." His subjects
include the "little stubborn people of the hill," "ironwood,"
"lean men" (poetically, lean men seem to go well with the hills
and fat men with the lowlands), hounds, sycamores, copper-
heads, dead men in "gray coats, blue coats," cedars and lime-
stone, and rabbits and rabbit hunters. The poem is much more
sophisticated in technique than, say, the Georgian poetry of the
early Frost in England, who was writing poems so general that
they could be either American or English. At this time Warren
is already learned in the ways of the intricate poets; but the
effect achieved, though more reserved and less innocent than
the poems of the early Frost, is not much more accomplished.

Some Blacks—Two Early Poems and a Sequel

In 1930 in *This Quarter,* published in Paris, Warren published
a poem that pictures the black cemetery in Guthrie, named
Vinegar Hill in truth and in poetry. From there, Warren says,
you can see "the supper smoke rise from Squiggtown"—also an
actual name for the black section of Guthrie. The lovers in
"Tryst on Vinegar Hill" are young blacks, making love among
the graves. The sky over the black cemetery, somehow absorb-
ing the spirits of the dead, is intimate and blue

>   As if from that especial spot it drew
>   A deep primeval clarity
>   Up from the heart and desperate sinew
>   Of niggers who once were buried there.

As they lie all night among the dead on Vinegar Hill, their
love-making even wakes the dead, who with envy and nostalgia "watch the lovers and . . . spread / Their fingers to the
little spark / Of warmth the living bodies own."

"Tryst on Vinegar Hill" and its young blacks have an earthy
zest that contrasts with such poetic characters as Dr. Knox and
Mr. Moody, as well as with the celibate friars and Prufrock-like

characters who at that time peopled the poems of Ransom and Tate.

Perhaps it is not surprising that Warren's poetic attention was attracted by a lynching in Guthrie. The source event of two of Warren's poems occurred when he was twenty-three, in young manhood, a few years after he had left Guthrie for education and then for his careers in the world.

Primus Kirby was lynched in Guthrie in the middle of June, 1926. His death left little record in the annals of history, but it is still indelibly written on the memories of those who live in Guthrie and who can remember events as long ago as 1926. All of them differ on a few details and forget a few, but all of them remember. Primus Kirby did not quietly approach his death or gently pass away. He had killed his wife, wounded an aunt, and shot a deputy named Ed Bringhurst. Then a mob efficiently put him to death.

Differences between journalistic accounts, folk memories, and poetic representations are striking. In a front-page editorial the Louisville *News* (19 June 1926) called the lynching "an act of sport a holiday festivity for a lot of small town ignorant, prejudiced whites—ignorant of the true fundamentals of law and order but not too ignorant to know they could kill a Negro with impuriety [impunity] and get by with it." Short factual reports appeared in the Brooklyn *Eagle,* a small Missouri paper, and the Atlanta *Constitution.* The Memphis *Commercial Appeal* (16 June 1926) stressed first the peace in town following the lynching, gave a fairly long and mostly factual report, and concluded with the opinion (or wish) that "A majority of the negroes in Guthrie were reported to be in accord with the hanging."[3]

The folks of Guthrie remember the crime and the capture, but their memories dwell on the events that followed. Some believe that the "law men" were the ones who carried out the lynching. One woman remembered that "the old nigger" (he was twenty-six) tried to hide behind her husband to avoid being shot as he was captured.[73] The sheriff and a deputy sheriff started driving Kirby to the county seat in Elkton, but they had agreed with local citizens on the route before they left

Guthrie, and they even selected a place where they would have car trouble. A half century later when I was talking with one of Warren's contemporaries, he wept in a tender elderly way about his mother's one-hundredth birthday party. But he remembered the lynching without apparent emotion. Four carloads of men arrived at the stalled car of the sheriff, took Kirby, tied the customary rope about his neck, threw the rope over the limb of a tree, and pulled him up by the rope. The sentimental old gentleman still remembers how they shot Kirby so many times that blood ran over the tops of his shoes. Later, when I had put away the tape cassette and the notepaper, he said, "I was in this hanging. I had my hand on the rope. I didn't believe in the shooting." Though choking by rope would surely be more painful than instant shooting, he apparently could endure brutality more easily than blood. Kent Greenfield, childhood friend of Warren, said that he was at the tree when they took the body down and that Primus Kirby had been shot so many times that bullets rolled out of his clothes.

When Kirby died, Robert Penn Warren was not in Guthrie. On July 2, 1926, about two weeks later, Warren wrote Donald Davidson that he was just "emerging" from the examinations of the third session at Berkeley in California; so he could not have been near enough to Primus Kirby and Guthrie to read anything but letters and national news. Probably a few details of the story came to him by hearsay and folklore. In 1926 Warren spent two days at Guthrie during the Christmas season. In 1927 he wrote Donald Davidson and enclosed a copy of his "latest poem, Pondy Woods" for appraisal and criticism. That version, Warren said, was "not the latest copy."[85] He had, then, been working carefully for some time on different versions of a poem about a lynching.

In the first collection of Warren's poems, *Selected Poems, 1923–1943,* "Pondy Woods" stands last except for two other poems (both of them about Todd County in some way). At the end of the Fugitive days or shortly thereafter, then, Warren was anticipating the return to his childhood settings that was to come in poems written twenty-five years later. Anyone from Todd County who read "Pondy Woods" would have immediately recognized details in the poem. Perhaps Warren's effective use of the country he knew so well was one reason why a critic as late as 1947–48 in the *American Oxonian* called "Pondy Woods" Warren's "most popular poem to date."[111]

The actual Pondy Woods was a large area ten to twelve miles deep, running from Guthrie and the Tennessee-Kentucky line to a tributary of the Cumberland River. The swamp, wet bushes, trees, and ponds made a good place for Warren's murderous black man to flee, although Primus Kirby did not himself have time to take that route before his arrest. Details of the swampy hiding place of Warren's Jim Todd are particular and true to that kind of landscape. There were "mud and muck," black-gum trees, a buzzard roost, a corduroy road, and water moccasins—an environment not unlike that of Faulkner's "Red Leaves." In Squiggtown (the "niggertown" of Guthrie), Warren's black man was lynched on Saturday. Folklore about the ecstasies and violence of blacks on Saturday led to the choice of that day of the week. In Guthrie literally, and in the poem, the saloon was named the Blue Goose. It had two halves, one for whiskey and one for a grocery store. And it stood on the state line; anyone fleeing the law could run into another state without going outdoors.[73]

"Pondy Woods" is more intriguing and learned than it is magnificently poetic. It reveals a young poet struggling to combine the materials of his childhood, the education and associations of his Fugitive days, and the learning he had been acquiring since the time of his childhood reading. It is a rich poem, but more experimental than successful. The Guthrie background is described in language derived from the styles and manners of the Fugitives. The poem is rather traditional and exhibits the Latinity natural to those who had an old-fashioned secondary education. The formal diction applied to earthy subjects is reminiscent of Ransom: buzzards "achieve the blue tense altitudes"; they are "black figments"; they "tilted down / A windless vortex"; they reveal "obscenity in form and grace." Big Jim Todd is less classical as he hides, listening for the sounds of "hoofs on the corduroy road" and "for the foul and sucking sound / A man's foot makes on the marshy ground." The words of a talking buzzard fall into a darkness described in polysyllables like Ransom's or Faulkner's: it is "mystic and ambrosial."

The buzzard talking Latin has evoked a none-too-friendly smile from the critics,[113] and even tolerant modern blacks object to the buzzard's "Nigger, your breed ain't metaphysical." But they forget that Warren, Tate, and Ransom, knowledgeable as they were of traditional poetry and talented as they were in the manners of sophisticated poets, were not admirers of intellectuals or metaphysical characters or men. Warren may have hoped that the conglomeration of styles and manners would reflect the situation of Jim Todd, fleeing lynchers in a swamp but dressed in "patent-leather shoes and Sunday clothes."

Warren's talking point of view, the buzzard (again after the manner of Ransom's ballad dialogue and his birds) is patronizing and at the same time learnedly aware of ancient contexts for the fleeing black man. He compares Jim Todd as victim to Jesus Christ: "The Jew-boy died. The Syrian vulture swung / Remotely above the cross whereon he hung." And twice he compares the black man's flight to Jesus's movements: "At dawn unto the Sabbath wheat he came . . .," and "To the ripe wheat fields he came at dawn." (Mark 2:23: "It came to pass, that he went through the corn fields on the sabbath day.")

In addition to the ballad and the religious contexts, there is also a classical allusion, as the garrulous buzzard reminds Jim Todd that *"Nom omnis moriar,"* quoting Horace's *Odes* (3.30.6); in Gordon Williams's translation, "I shall not all die." For a moment in the poem Horace seems to echo some of the promises of Jesus. And, it is said, "Jim understood." Here there is also an elusive reference to an American context: "Northward the printed smoke stood quiet above / The distant cabins of Squiggtown." The scene, "printed," partakes of the attributes of a lithograph perhaps, say, by Currier and Ives. Jim Todd, the doomed man, is literally and mythically a part of the American scene. His hearing also brings him abruptly back to the reality of the railroad town of Guthrie: "A train's far whistle blew and drifted away."

Within a context that seems incredibly complicated compared to the simplicity that many attribute to Warren, the poet has presented the story of a black man pursued by lynchers, but he has not created a posse, the lynching, a political or racial point of view—anything that would make the situation political or public. The poem applies all its myth to the black man's spree, his flight, and the terrors he must confront. It was a rather strange work to send for suggestions to the archetypal Southern conservative, Donald Davidson; and certainly it is noncommittal and obscurely compact for the author of "The Briar Patch" in *I'll Take My Stand*—that essay on the Negro in the South and the modern world.

"Pondy Woods" is a remarkable example of a poet's mind practicing a variety of techniques, but its allusions and manners and meanings fail to come together into a striking and singular whole. The poet does not succeed in lifting the man into the mythical and religious contexts that he created. M. L. Rosenthal believes that Jim Todd epitomizes "the nameless guilt and unearned doom of all humanity."[113] Perhaps that is something of what Warren wished to achieve, but the buzzard ("a buzzard can smell the thing you've done") suggests that Jim Todd's guilt, though nameless, is real.

"Pondy Woods" was written not long after the actual event, and Warren then printed the poem and filed away the story of the lynching for at least forty years in the back of his mind. But it surfaced again, as the deaths of the prototypes of Joe Christmas and the heroic black man in Faulkner's "Pantaloon in Black" and the shooting of the black man gone mad in Wolfe's "Child by Tiger" came back to the minds of the authors decades after all the blood had dried.

The memory of Primus Kirby came back to Warren in a poem in *Or Else—Poem/Poems 1968–1974.* "Ballad of Mister Dutcher and the Last Lynching in Gupton" resurrects the old story with a different point of view, switching from the story of the victim to that of the victimizer. In the life of Primus Kirby there were many lynchers, but in the second poem the poet concentrates on one man, the leader. In the nature of man and lynchings and anonymous crimes, the head of the mob is one never to be talked about. Besides the man who told me that he had his hand on the rope and Kent Greenfield's memory of seeing the riddled body taken down, I have heard of only one

other observer or participant. He is the vaguest, the most anonymous of all. One man who "lived on the edge of town for a
while," I am told, "did most of the hanging in Guthrie."
Whose? And how many? No one may know. If some do, they
will not tell, and when they do talk, they do not tell all.

The first stanza of Warren's poem catches astutely the
anonymity of this leader of the guilty. His character is, most of
all, timeless. Like the Wandering Jew or Satan, "he must have
been just as old in / days when young as later." His face is gray
—without color. His eyes are not even gray, but "that color
there's not even a / name for"—they lack even the identity of
black or white. His coat is gray, and his house, and his smile.
His actions are as much without humanity as the other things
are without color. Utterly ensnared in routine, he goes "twice
a day to the depot," "twice a day . . . home," the latter to eat
and "to shut / the door of his small gray house." His words
seem not to exist either. Whatever he said "you never quite
caught." If that "gray smile" is a facial movement, it is hardly
a smile at all. It is "turned more inside than out." It is a response,
Warren suggests, to the man himself instead of to the one who
greeted him. It is a recollection and a revelation (but only to
himself) of what he did in the last lynching in Gupton.

In another of Warren's poems, Big Billie Potts, the frontier
innkeeper, murderer and robber, had a wife who was "dark and
little," and "nobody knew what was in her head." But she is
dark, or evil, not gray, not a memory of evil. A partner of evil,
Mister Dutcher's wife is small too, but she is not dark, but gray.
Her face is gray, and her gingham, and coat. The gray-faced pair
reside together in the gray house, but Mister Dutcher at night
stares up to "where / dark hid the ceiling." The darkness of
time may obscure the fact of his old crime, but Mister Dutcher
still smiles, in mystery or irony, at the ignorance of those who
will only speculate about the evil of the man who lived on the
edge of town. His wife and his son, both "gray-faced," die, and
at last Mister Dutcher reveals what he has known. The telling
is more important than the listener or the story. Warren does
not say how Mister Dutcher opened his heart. He "brought it
forth." What Mister Dutcher had carried around in his head is

the same thing that members of Percy Grimm's company in *Light in August* carried for so many years in theirs. Neither Faulkner nor Warren names what it is. Faulkner's characters have something "in their memories forever and ever" that "they are not to lose. . . , in whatever peaceful valleys, beside whatever placid and reassuring streams of old age. . . . It will be there, musing, quiet, steadfast, not fading and not particularly threatful, but of itself alone serene, of itself alone triumphant."

Mister Dutcher may try to lose it; at least "he, in the fullness of time, and / in glory, brought it forth." With a few alterations he tells the story of the lynching of Primus Kirby, alias Jim Todd in the earlier poem. Again he shoots a representative of the law and tries to flee. But the "Ballad of Mister Dutcher" reports the details of the death of Primus Kirby, and "Pondy Woods" describes only his flight. The constable drives in a way to be caught:

> The constable, it sort of seemed,
> had car trouble, and there he was
> by the road, in the cooling shade
> of a big white oak, with his head
> stuck under the hood and a wrench
> in his hand.

The "small gray-faced man" ties the rope into the hangman's noose. The constable has car trouble at the arranged place, and the black man dies from bullets before he can choke from the hanging.

In all the grayness of Mister Dutcher's character, the lynching is his one way to gain identity. It is "that one talent kept," as Warren says, "against the / advice of Jesus, wrapped in a napkin, and death to hide." Indeed, the lynching itself does not provide Mister Dutcher a lasting identity. He is not allowed the "contumely, wrath, hurt ego, and / biologic despair" that is the "darkness that . . . is Time." It could be in the poem that only the poet remembers his name because the anonymity of the hellish crime of lynching produces an unnameable reaction that lacks even the specificity of guilt. Read thus, the poem is a meditation on the ironical and quiet and gray effects of the lynching on the lyncher. But Warren recalls that he lynched *because* of the grayness, not that it was a result. Warren comments: "Maybe Mr. Dutcher's 'grayness' made him a lyncher because of the lack of identity, the hurt."

In the "Ballad of Mister Dutcher" the poet speculates on whether he will try "to locate / where that black man got buried, though / that would, of course, be somewhat difficult." Graves of blacks often remained unmarked.

The "Ballad of Mister Dutcher" is more ballad than learned poem, but it is also literary as well as traditional. The stanzas and the poetic form in general do follow the traditional ballad form. Warren could have used conceits, classical allusions, Biblical contexts, and the elaborate techniques of "Pondy Woods." But except for an occasional phrase ("the fullness of time") and the reference to the Biblical parable of the talents, Warren did not avail himself of elaborate poetic devices. To convey the folk situation, he uses dialect and trite language and traditional Southern humor.

He remembers hearing details of the events in Guthrie, but says that he never tried to "track down" the lynching because it was not his actual subject.

"The black tried to stick up a likker store in Hopkinsville," Warren heard, "and shot the operator and hopped a freight train bound for Guthrie. Telephone calls ahead flagged the train down for a waiting posse. The criminal shot a member of the posse, and was taken into Guthrie. Then a lynching was planned (sometimes said to be in connivance with the law and a car supposed to be broken down)."[95]

> One hot
> afternoon in Hoptown, some fool
> nigger, wall-eyed drunk and with a
> four-bit hand-gun, tried to stick up
> a liquor store, shot the clerk, and,
> still broke, grabbed a freight, and was high-
> tailing for Gupton, in happy
> ignorance that the telephone
> had ever been invented.

Mr. Dutcher takes the lynching rope when it is brought, and

> Quick as a wink, six turns
> around the leader, the end snubbed,
> and there was that neat cylinder
> of rope the noose line could slide through
> easy as a greased piston or
> the dose of salts through the widow-
> woman. . . .

The folkish and light-hearted tone ironically conveys the re-
puted light-heartedness of an old-time Southern lynching. It is
intended almost to slip up on the reader and to offend with
language appropriate to the temporary mood of the lynchers
and contradictory to the life of Mr. Dutcher when he is not
engaged in the great event of his life. Ballad though it is, the
poetic narrative of Mister Dutcher is lyrical and dramatic. The
images dominated by gray create dramatically the mind of the
man, of his small gray wife who has to live with him, and of
the "one gray-faced son." (Warren comments that "the son,
rather bright and talented, became a mechanic, then drunkard;
picked up in the snow, drunk, one night, he died in jail. I think
this is right. Our boyhood friendship was based on his electrical
and mechanical expertise."[95]) The grayness of their lives begins
the poem and establishes the tone, which reveals the last effect
on the character, and vicariously on the reader, of the horrors
of the hanging of the black man. The ballad, dramatic and
lyrical, ends with the oblivion of the lost grave of the victim of
the mob. The "Ballad of Mister Dutcher and the Last Lynching
in Gupton" is strikingly local and Southern, but it raises (or
lowers) the situation to a universal despair.

Separated by the great span of years, Warren's two poems
differ greatly in method: one draws mainly on a formal literary
tradition and the other has a folkish vehicle. The two poems
seem to telescope the history of racial violence in the South and
at the same time to embody it in the experiences of the two
victims, in one poem the lynched man, and the leader of the
lynchers in the other. Perhaps by coincidence and perhaps

partly by design, the two poems together serve as a meditation on history. The criminals are all victimizers and victims. Even their tombstones are forgotten unless the poet can rediscover them. One died in violence and blood, and one died in grayness of soul. Perhaps history will consign the crime, the pain, and the guilt to oblivion, but at any time someone may seek out the artifacts and reminders. The poet may find them and meditate. What now shall he say of the energy and the despair of Pondy Woods and what of the grayness of the last lyncher in Gupton?

Years Without Poems and the New Beginnings

The first accomplished poem with distinctly country and Kentucky character and origins was "The Ballad of Billie Potts" (1943), but for at least a decade it was also the last poem of any kind ever finished, as Warren has pointed out many times. This ballad was based on an ancient Kentucky story of frontier robbers and filicide. Warren first heard a garbled version of the story from his Great-Aunt Anna (his Grandfather Penn's sister-in-law), who told the story with a setting in the "land between the rivers"—wild country between the Cumberland and the Tennessee. It is not a poem derived from the poet's childhood. Except for the book-length *Brother to Dragons,* there were no more poems until *Promises,* and when that volume appeared Warren's character as a poet had changed. *Promises* is family poetry, much of it based on Warren's relationship to his wife and children. But several of the poems derive from life in Guthrie and Cerulean: "Country Burying (1919)," "School Lesson Based on Word of Tragic Death of Entire Gillum Family," "Dragon Country: To Jacob Boehme," and "Boy's Will, Joyful Labor without Pay, and Harvest Home (1918)." The setting and some narrative events of other poems are based on childhood scenes, though a little more generally: "What Was the Promise that Smiled . . . ?" "Court-Martial," "Gold Glade," "Dark Woods," "Dark Night of," and "Walk by Moonlight. . . ."

"Boyhood in Tobacco Country," first collected in *Being Here,* is a mood poem about memories of curing tobacco in the autumn in Todd or Trigg county. A red sunset, black groves of trees, curing barns, and their smoke establish the background for "a black / Voice, deeper and bluer than sea-heart, swee-ter / Than sadness or sorghum" as it "utters the namelessness / Of life to the birth of a first star." The poem ends with meditation on a similar but much later twilight which provokes both grief and joy.

The poems about Warren's childhood in *Promises* are rather long, they are more about the local childhood setting than any poems written before, and the trend they establish is indeed significant. In the period 1954–1956, Warren redefined his en-tire method of writing a poem. The very beginning of a short poem, the basic conception, assumed a different form for him, he has said; and in turn his method of conceiving a poem resulted in a different kind of poetry. The way a poem seemed to pop into his mind without conscious plan ultimately defined the subject matter, the development, and the meaning. Before, he had had "too abstract a view of what constituted the germ of a poem *for me.* "[33] In this new period poems began to proceed from a particular concrete thing, whereas the earlier ones at least seem to have derived from a concept, to have begun as a sort of idea of what a poem would be, what its subject would be. I suspect that Warren as a young poet before "Billie Potts" in 1943 started with meanings and then found images, that as an older poet he found an image and in some fashion let it work out its own meaning. Now, he says, "The poetry tends to take off from the essential narrative, see. . . . I began more and more to find the germs of poems in a small romance, in a small cryptic piece of brutal reality, you see, rather than from abstraction. The later poems take off from some episode, a reality, actuality, I mean."[95]

The new poems were "more directly tied to a realistic base of facts . . . , an event, an anecdote, an observation." They were not rigidly "autobiographical," but they had "literal germs"— perhaps an autobiographical beginning from which Warren might stray as he thought about the poem and then wrote it. The new poems (Warren insists on the point in an interview with Richard B. Sale) "were tied closer to the texture of casual life, incidental life, incidental observations, direct experience."[33] *Incidental* seems to suggest the way a subject occurred to Warren, ways of the imagination that are recognizable to a passive and receptive self but not altogether subject to the conscious mind.

In the manuscripts of *Promises* one piece is called "Todd County Dragon: to Jacob Boehme."[94] The poem survived without a great many revisions, but the title was changed and generalized to "Dragon Country: To Jacob Boehme." The difference between the two titles is significant. Warren began writing the poem in terms of the particularity of his county. He published it as a poem about any and all countries that may still believe in dragons and other supernatural manifestations, though within the poem he retained the name of Todd County. The new title recognizes that the poem is about not only Todd County but also Kentucky or, more, the South, or, even more, any rural or folk or country world where such beliefs survive.

In one sense, the factual, there was never to my knowledge any Todd County dragon, nor any stories about one. No person I talked to recalls the destruction Warren describes of Jack Simms' hog pen, or the disappearance of a salesman—or his body—after an accident. No one that I know in Guthrie remembers Jebb Johnson's or anyone else's boot "with the leg, what was left, inside." But in countries that have dragons and such beasts in the hogpen or in the mind, some call the universal fear a painter or panther or cattymount, a bear, or some unseen creature whose cries are more terrible than the sounds of owls at night. There are Indian caves and devil's dens and places haunted by unnameable fears. There is a difference between the dragons of the country and those of the city. Son of Sam, a murderer in Brooklyn, caused awesome fear, but eventually he was detected and tried and disposed of in the courts and in human institutions. He was somewhere in the flesh—a thing to be hunted and found. But civilization can never deal with the dragons of the country, those of the mind and the spirit.

Warren's dragon leaves signs but is not seen. Like a vast snail or slug, he leaves slime in his path on the railroad tracks, and "his great turd steams" in the fields of the morning. He tears up hog pens, scares mules who tear up a wagon. But men cannot "bring to bay / That belly-dragging earth-evil." People disappear, sometimes leaving a limb, sometimes not. Relatives lie and thus deny the existence of the dragon in their lives. The immediate terror is so great that the people forget the great fears of the world, the "maneuvers of Russia, or other great powers."

A religious revival does not come to "the point," because "we are human, and the human heart / Demands language for reality that has not the slightest dependence / On desire, or need." The poem, however, is dedicated to Jacob Boehme, an early Lutheran mystic who believed in the existence of evil and good in the world and the flesh as well as in the spirit. A Protestant mystic appropriate for Warren's area of the South, Boehme saw the divine and demonic in the daily reality of his sixteenth-century world. In his first vision of a manifestation, he saw "the sun's rays in a bright pewter dish" and attained an "inward ecstacy." The spirit is revealed by the material: "The outward spirit and body was unto the inward as a *wonder* of Divine manifestation." Similarly, evil is also embodied in the physical.[112] Thus everyman's heart is dragon country as well as possibly God's country.

The community cannot "in great hunts" destroy the evil, the dragon. The beast wreaks its devastation on that country; it exists as evil in Boehme's supernatural terms. Although the governor strives hard to confront the dragon and they call him "Saint George of Kentucky," institutional man cannot cope with the supernatural problem. Thus Warren combines many traditional areas of experience: Southern tall tales and humor, folk beliefs, the real and the imagined world of Kentucky, even the flight to Akron or Detroit. There is also another world, which exists only by implication and, poetically, almost entirely outside the poem. If there is "dragon country," there is also, one must know, country that does not believe in dragons. This world appears briefly in the philosophical last stanza: "But if the Beast were withdrawn now, life might dwindle again / To the ennui, the pleasure, and night sweat. . . ." Warren suggests that the Supernatural appears with the capitalization and with the suggestion that the Beast is a manifestation of some still more terrible Thing ("withdrawn"—something has a leash on

the dragon). In the worlds without dragons, life has dwindled
and there is ennui, or the nothingness which, according to Eliot,
is greater than Evil itself.

Boyhood

Boys in a town like Guthrie, surrounded by a countryside of
farms, do home work, town work, and occasionally field work.
When Red Warren wanted to, he worked for pay in the fields
at harvest time for his grandfather in Cerulean. In the summer
he built bridges or cut dogwood for the Litchfield Spindle Company of Connecticut. This last was, he says, "a hell of a job with
a hand axe or a short saw in humid swamps and high tempera-
tures." Mostly he worked at such jobs "with the idea of tough-
ening my scrawny self."[95] A four-part poem in *Promises*, "Boy's
Will, Joyful Labor without Pay, and Harvest Home (1918),"
describes labor in the fields as effectively as Frost (say, especially, in "The Code"). It is a poem more exactly detailed in its
imagery of the wheat harvest than one of Ransom's greatest but
most symbolic poems, "Antique Harvesters." Warren's philosophical observations are present but rather subdued compared
to the meanings of "Dragon Country." "Boy's Will" progresses
from a breakfast of oatmeal to the work of the morning. Bark-
ing dogs follow an old steam tractor and the workers to the
field. In the last part of the poem the laborers are paid at the
end of the long day. Work for Warren, he says, was "play";
for the regular hands, it was daily bread. The day is pleasant,
and the vigor of early morning starts the boy to working too
hard. Even the strong wagoner who stacks the hay in the
wagon warns him, " 'Boy, save yore strength, 'fore you got
none left.' "
    The central and most impressive image of the poem comes
in the center of the work and the heat of the day. The smaller
animals like field mice and rabbits flee, but that eternal enemy
of man since the Garden of Eden—the snake—stands his
ground and suffers his doom. "Defiant, tall in that blast of
day, / Now eye for eye, he swaps his stare. / His outrage glit-
ters on the air." The poem and the tone empathize with the

snake, but in the Biblical tradition the workers "bruise" his head. Despite his defiance and his rearing up, the big black snake is "snagged high on a pitchfork tine," where he makes "slow arabesques till the bullbats wake." One man spits and says, "Hell, just another snake." Perhaps, by implication, so are we all "just another" of our own species. The snake's defiance as he rears from his earthen home and the grace in his slow arabesque elevate him above the Biblical level assigned him. But pity for the snake and commentary on the nature of creatures and of man remain implicit only in the images.

The fourth part of the poem ends the day of labor with hand tools and steam tractors in the field. Six stanzas of this part stop the thresher, come home from the field, put a farm hand to bed "too sleepy now to wash himself," watch the farm and its creatures settle down, and return to the image "In the star-pale field [where], the propped pitchfork lifts / its burden hung black, to the white star." In the last two stanzas the youth has grown older and meditative. He names "each item, but cannot think / What ... they must mean." He remembers with "a heart-stab blessed past joy or despair," but that snake he remembers is not named. The poet—unusual for Warren—does not define the various circumferences of the meanings or the limitations. Somehow the dead snake seems to suggest the limitations of all creatures of the earth, and the magnificence of their failing struggle. That is a major note of the poem, but perhaps the description of the youth's work in the field surpasses all attempts to define a meaning.

At first glance, "When Life Begins," from *Being Here,* seems implausible. The early stanzas seem ordinary, comfortable, the lazy dream-prosaic life under the shade of the cedar tree looking at the far horizon. The cob pipe and the jeans and the place belong to Gabriel Thomas Penn, frequent subject of Warren's talk and of the poems. To him the boy attributes all wisdom and experience. The love of the grandfather, the boy's admiration of his wisdom, the character of old man and boy in other poems, and the general tone that describes the company of youth and age suggest that the boy is in early adolescence—a time when he would contemplate sexuality in silence or in clandestine masturbation.

The peace, quiet, and reverie are interrupted first by the grandfather's turning as he often does to his memories of the War and of some drastic event that seems to illuminate a particular meaning. One stanza recreates the clamor of war: skirmishers, rifle-fire, shell bursts. Then the violence is succeeded by the earlier quiet of the farm and the grandfather and the boy. "In the country-quiet, momentarily / After that event renewed, one lone / Quail calls."

The recollections of war, however, have awakened the old man to the complexities and puzzlements of life and its meanings and its violence. No quail call can make him forget the human drama of the war and of the particular incident which on this occasion sticks in his mind. So he tells his grandson (or he thinks aloud) about the death of a boy-soldier; he describes "How a young boy, dying, broke into tears. / 'Ain't scairt to die'—the boy's words—'it's jist / I ne'er had no chance to know what tail's like.' " Perhaps forgetful of his grandson, reminded of the death of the youth and of the war, the grandfather drifts on to memories of the fulfillment of his life, which the dead young soldier never attained. He remembers his long-dead wife and the romance of their marriage. He recalls his love in terms less overtly sexual than those of the dying young: " 'My Mary, her hands were like silk, / But strong—and her mount on his shadow would dance.' / Once said: 'But things—they can seem like a dream.' " Remembering how the mount danced on his shadow, he dreams for the second time—this time of a relationship fulfilled—not of the unknowing and innocent but lustful wish for a piece of tail. But the dead youth, his wish, the war, the old man's beloved wife, and all the past fade away. Everything turns to the moment under the cedars with the grandson.

> Old eyelids shut the horizon out.
> The boy sat and wondered when life would begin,
> Nor knew that, beyond the horizon's heave,
> Time crouched, like a great cat, motionless
> But for tail's twitch. Night comes. Eyes glare.

In a sense the Confederate soldier and the listening grandson share the same wonderment: "when life would begin" and what it would be. The old may puzzle about meanings and negligently tell enigmatic, brutal, or frank anecdotes before the young. It is not surprising that the grandson listens intently to such a story of violence, death, and sexuality. He wonders about his own life after he has heard the meditative and quiet grandfather tell a stark story of how a boy just older than his grandson confronted ultimate meanings and the ultimate end.

The main thrust of the boy's last words is not that he dies with a hard on, simultaneously wishing to tear off a piece of tail and heaving his last breath. It is not really a question of lust. Indeed, the lust and the satisfaction of the lust have both become impossible. That is, the aim of man is to know. And one of the most intense forms of knowledge is to know the human experience of physical and lustful love. It is an urge put well in James Dickey's "The Sheep Child" when he describes the "Farm boys wild to couple / with anything   with soft-wooded trees / With mounds of earth   mounds / Of pine-straw." It is the biological, psychological, spiritual, innocent urge to know. It surpasses the desire to die with the boots on or to die with a hard on. It attains an ultimate mystery. Who is to define the plausibility of mystery? The poet. But he does not define it; he makes it. Difficult as the task is, unprovable as the judgment must remain, it seems to me that Warren has made a marvelous and mysterious poem out of the materials of the wonderment of the grandfather, the heroism and the incompleteness of the soldier, and the anticipation of the boy about his own life as he listens to the grandsire's story of the other boy. Ultimately, the question is as mysterious as the question of mental processes of a baby or of Benjy Compson or of the hallucinations of a dying person. What may seem to be implausible in the bare facts of the matter can be great poetry without any rational or material measuring stick of any kind.

"Dark Night of the Soul" resembles in poetry one of Warren's short stories, "Blackberry Winter," which has become an American classic. The persona recollects that he was twelve—nine in the short story—when a tramp came, and he sees a man appear from the woods, move "without truth or dimension / A-cross that vast space men should shun." Later in the afternoon, the boy goes for the cows and sees "beneath elder bloom, the eyes glare." The tramp flees, and later that night the boy thinks how the tramp moves

> by the unremitting glory of stars high in
> the night heavens there.
> He moves in joy past contumely of stars or insolent indifference
> of the dark air.
>
> May we all at last enter into that awfulness of joy he has found
> there.

But what has he found? No suggestions are provided by the poem except perhaps understanding, isolation, and the lack of a need for knowledge that cannot be attained.

Some of the poems in *Now and Then* return to the fundamentals of the older times in the South. "Amazing Grace in the Back Country" is one of Warren's most remarkable works; few short poems pull together successfully such diverse elements. Most of his vignettes of Guthrie and Cerulean focus with the intensity of a laser beam on one central event and a few surrounding details, and they end with a subjective and philosophical point toward which the entire poem has been driving. "Amazing Grace" presents two distinct and even opposite worlds, which nevertheless share a good many of the same attributes.

A common sight on the rural Southern landscape even in modern times is a small revivalist tent pitched at the edge of town. Sometimes the tent is erected by the greed of hypocritical money-collecting preachers, perhaps more often by the fervor of a fanatical revivalist. Warren names the season of revivals ("late August"), and describes where the tent had been pitched "There by woods, where oaks of the old forest-time / Yet swaggered and hulked over upstarts." The last eleven lines of the first stanza are an elaborate comparison—partly figurative—of the revivalist's tent and the absurd world of a traveling carnival and the attendant freaks.

Such carnivals attract curious crowds by appealing to human attraction to the repulsively inhuman. Eudora Welty is well acquainted with that world, as is shown by her account of the petrified man and of the geek, the little black man who passed as Keela, an Indian maiden, who ate live chickens. Carnival attractions are abnormal, deformed in mind or body, unable to follow a customary way of life and to attain any kind of fulfillment. They are freaks who attract ticket-buyers.

Warren's carnival contains human beings in some extreme condition ("fat lady, human skeleton, geek, / Man-woman"). In most carnivals, the last, a hermaphrodite with the sexual organs of both man and woman, usually goes through something like a parody of a strip tease, with the audience paying more admission with each new revelation. The last and ultimate step sometimes separates the men and the women while the freak talks in pretended medical or professional tones of the disappointments—or joys—of his and her double life. Animals too are in the show—a "moth-eaten lion" and a boa constrictor that eats a young calf. A herpetologist (Peter Lindsey, of the Atlanta Zoo) tells me that no boa could eat a calf, that only a python or some other larger species of snake could—one that can swallow an animal larger than the snake is. That also seems freakish, natural as it is, and violently repulsive. The poem also includes a type that always seems to accompany such a carnival: "whores to whom menopause now / Was barely a memory" and who "leave / A new and guaranteed brand of syphilis handy."

But the true carnival is a "tabernacle / To the glory of God the Most High." The persona, like the little boy in Flannery O'Connor's "The River," aged twelve, hears a fundamentalist preacher, "an ex-railroad engineer," threaten of hell and promise paradise for the few, "Eyes a-glaze with the mania of joy." The youth is asked to come to the mourner's bench to weep about his sins and cry out his immediate need for salvation, assisted by "some old-fool dame / In worn-out black silk." But in all the years he never gets there. He flees. Like one of Jonathan Edwards's sinners in the hands of an angry God, after a brief time of mourning, he "hardened his heart, / Like a flint nigger-head rounded slick in a creek-bed." He runs out of the tent, the temple of God, and leans against a tree and vomits. He flees from the tent because it cannot provide him with the salvation he needs, but he still knows the damnation of his human condition, whether in religious terms or not. Many of the mourners attain amazing grace, but not the boy.

The poem is a reminiscence so true that one knows it happened to thousands of souls, whether or not to Warren. Hours after the saved and the damned have gone home, the boy "lay / Wondering and wondering how many / A morning would I rise up to greet, / And what grace find." In a figurative but perhaps agonizing sense, the boy, grown old, still lies by the spring and wonders about the state of his soul in a world, natural and supernatural, that goes on through an indeterminable number of mornings. He has not received an amazing abundance of grace, but he is (like his creator Warren) a yearner, and he still quietly desires the salvation wept for on the mourner's bench in the revivalist's tent. The spiritual desires began in the tent "long years ago. I was twelve years old then." The poem ardently expresses in quiet and beautiful poetry all the intensity of the folk religion. The unfulfillment of the carnival freaks, the violence of the animals, the strangeness of their condition in their world prepare for the strangeness of the revivalists and even for the strong yearnings of the boy or any soul who longs for the certainty of amazing grace. The vehicle may be the back country of the South, and certainly it is the back country of the remote recesses of the soul. In few of Warren's poems is there a more perfect blending of the materials of his childhood origins and the meanings of his philosophical searchings. Perhaps the older poem, "Original Sin," is a better poem by the earlier formalist standards, but "Amazing Grace" takes the materials of what is usually the caricatured South and elevates them to the level of the questions of Job.

Some Townspeople

Warren was not pleased enough with "So You Agree with What I Say? Well, What Did I Say?" to admit it to his next *Selected Poems.* When I told him that I disagreed with his decision, that I thought he had neglected a wonderful poem, he disarmingly agreed. "No, no, no, no. I shouldn't have left him

[Mr. Moody] out. . . . He was an albino, cobbler, a retired old bachelor. And he knew the Bible by heart."[95] *You, Emperors, and Others* includes a few other historical poems about both the American past and the past of classical history. But except in "Mortmain" probably there is some truth in Warren's judgment that this volume is inferior, and certainly the narratives that extend the portraits of the imagined town are subordinated at this time.

"So You Agree . . ." is a portrait of one of the most solitary and most self-sufficient characters in all of the works. In January 1966, Warren wrote Allen Tate that "So You Agree . . ." is "about old Mr. Moody at Guthrie."[92] So far as I can tell, Mr. Moody has disappeared from the significant written records of man—except in Warren's poem. Several old-timers in Guthrie remember him and his manner of living—if living it was. Seemingly a man with only a very little meaning in his life to hold to, Mr. Moody clung tenaciously to what he had, and those who knew him (in life as in Warren's poem) meditated on his emptiness.

Mr. Moody of Guthrie was a man of peculiar ways. He was a hermit, a man who lived alone, plied his little trade in a dirty shop, and strayed quietly and unknown through the streets of his little town. Half blind, the people say, he was an albino. Although he read the Bible a lot and went to the Methodist Church in Guthrie, he tried—old goat that he was—to corner the girls and kiss them. And sometimes he succeeded. (Warren says that he has never heard this story about him.) He ate store-bought bread and the kinds of beans and meats that come straight from a can without passing near a stove. He was a cobbler, and he bottomed chairs—not much of a living in that. And nobody knew what was in his head.

Well, what did Mr. Moody say, as the title asks, or think? Nobody that I met in Guthrie knew. After Warren asks the question in the title, the poem declares that nobody knows what Mr. Moody meant. In poetry also the old man is "albino-pale, half-blind." His "orbit" (a set and unchanging ellipse) of life "revolved / Between his Bible and the cobbler's bench." Mr. Moody, apparently, has resolved "all human complexities" with his Bible, which has given him "Hope [capitalized for divinity, I take it] past deprivation, or any heart-wrench." But Warren casts doubt on the Hope. He adds, "Or so it seemed." The boys peep into the shack at dusk, watch the old man eat pork and beans and bread, light his old kerosene lamp, and read his book in the dim light.

Whether Mr. Moody bottomed chairs, as Kent Greenfield remembers, or repaired shoes, it is of little literary significance. Perhaps he even did both. The point poetically is that he worked at a lonely task with his hands. He could carry on his craft and at the same time meditate on his Bible, the mysteries of the men he saw, and the analogies between what he read in the good book and what he saw passing by in the town. Kent Greenfield told me of impressions reported and created in the poem. He lived by himself. Always he sat on the front seat of the church—an indication of intensity or anxiety, perhaps. He was an albino with pink eyes, a condition to make a man think, and (extraneous to the facts but not the sense of the poem) every member of his family had died of cancer. Kent also remembers that Mr. Moody was "a great Bible reader." His sister, Mattie, taught Kent. Although he ate pork and beans and bread, as in the poem, the sparse fare was not attributable to poverty: Mr. Moody owned two houses. Always he was in a hurry as he passed the field where the boys played baseball. (Kent mentioned his walking before I told him that Warren had written about it in the poem.)[19]

Now Mr. Moody is dead, but the poet thinks of him yet, as well as the boys who have died too and those who have gone on to "proper successes . . . / And made contribution to social and scientific improvements." Mr. Moody's life, his reading the Bible, and the "scientific improvements" of later times bring the poet to a puzzling conclusion in the last three lines of the poem: "If God short-changed Mr. Moody, it's time for Him / To give up this godding business, and make way / For somebody else to try, or an IBM." What a note of despair! It seems hopeless, but it is not the numbness of a skeptic resolved to make the best of his skepticism. It is an angry cry—anger against God *or* the lack of Him. It is the cry of what Warren calls himself, a yearner. Without God, there is little, but there is hope—no matter how little—of "somebody else" or an "IBM" machine. These are nothing more nor less than yearnings for the God Mr. Moody strove for and the poem seeks.

Well, as the title asks, "What Did I Say?" Or, what did the poem say? Really, nothing, or little more than nothing at all, as it promised nothing. We do not know that God short-changed Mr. Moody—or that He did not. Something, however, probably Mr. Moody's quiet orbit, did raise the question. And if there is a God with anything like the meaning denoted by the capitalized *Him,* there is no way for Him "To give up this godding business." Strange thought, but if there is a God, he is stuck with what He is and what He has done. And if He cannot give up the "godding," there is no way for somebody else to try to take it away. Now an IBM, a computer, the mechanized brains of the world might. But that is not a new suggestion by Warren or even for this century. If something like an IBM is to do the godding, that means it always has been the force in power. The world, in this case, is a mechanical force that runs by the materialistic laws of science. It makes the laws, puts Mr. Moody in his monotonous orbit, and leads him to bottom chairs (or repair shoes) and read the Bible. But that is not Warren's belief either. He reaches no conclusion in the poem about Mr. Moody and others in the world deprived of the fullness of life. Finally, the poem ends as it began with the title. "So You Agree with What I Say? Well, What Did I Say?" The poet asks the question. The portrait of Mr. Moody is a deeply religious question, but it is not affirmation—nor is it denial. "What Did I Say?" The community has provided setting, character, and images. But the people, Mr. Moody, and all the world have not said anything.

All of the poems of "Tale of Time" are about Warren's mother. In one he reveals her by showing how an insane druggist loved her so much that he told her his thoughts about the evil persons of the town. He loved a good woman because she was kind, but he responded with madness to the customers he regarded as unworthy of life. So he made plans—and they took him away to the insane asylum in Hopkinsville.

They put him in Hoptown, where he kept on making his list—
The same list he had on the street when he stopped my mother to
    say:
"Here they are, Miss Ruth, the folks that wouldn't be missed.

"Or this god-durn town would be lucky to miss,
If when I fixed a prescription I just happened to pour
Something in by way of improvement."

He kept a list of those he could poison and thereby do good for
the world. The man and the poetic situation are real. Indeed, I
am told that one druggist in Guthrie was a "very smart person,"
and he would talk about people that the town could do without.[73] Warren's mother told her son this story and about "the
promise to spare her and her family" (RPW on ms.). He "had
a problem"—alcohol and probably drugs. And, one may con-
clude, a problem of the soul. He took something for his nerves,
and they "carried him away" to the state hospital in Hopkinsville, which was called Hoptown in the community and the
poem (RPW on ms.). Warren told me the story in meditative
prose instead of in poetry. In Warren's talk repetition is
strongly indicative of the process of recalling and simultaneous
reflection on the event or person and on the poem at the same
moment. He said, "That's true, that's true, that's true. . . . He
said, 'I've got a list I'm going to show you. I'm going to fix. I'm
going to kill them.' But he never killed anybody."[21] In an interview with Edwin Newman, Warren added that the druggist did
make the list and that he did show it to Warren's mother:
" 'Miss Ruth,' he said, 'your name isn't on it. I always liked
you.' When committed to an institution, he kept on making his
list, the same list he had on the street."[22]
    That "list-maker," Warren says, "had the wit to see" that
Miss Ruth "was too precious to die." He saw dragons, but he
saw, also, in the woman a manifestation of a Spirit, the good
Will of Jacob Boehme. The poem ends with the reminder,
which one would expect in the last stanza of one of these
poems, that not all grasp the good Will—not "the attending
physician, nor God, nor I." Crazy as he was, the "mad druggist"
had a vision of both.

Some Tragedies

The patterns of many of the poems about Kentucky—memories of childhood, exact use of images and some general following of stories from Cerulean and Guthrie, a despairing or a questioning view of life and its meanings (or the lack of them), violence, sometimes an amazing solitude or quietness, the response of sensitive minds to desperate situations—are repeated in "School Lesson Based on Word of Tragic Death of Entire Gillum Family." The pun on lesson in the title is strong, perhaps even a little deliberately heavy-handed. The poem is about mass murder and suicide—certainly a subject designed to impress even the least responsive of students; and that may be a sufficient justification for the poet's "lesson." "The event," Warren says, "actually happened. . . . strong effect on school when evil came."[95]

Kent Greenfield's memory could invent, embroider, or forget. He told a story rather like that of the Gillums, containing elements that Warren may have remembered. A man by the name of Millen (other persons recall it as Milum or Millum) used an ax (Warren changed it to an ice-pick for effect) to kill four people—his brother and his sister-in-law, his mother and his father.[95] He killed his mother in the kitchen, his father on the back porch, his sister-in-law as she was making up the bed (after the blow she just fell across the bed), and finally he killed his brother. Then he prepared a place to attach a rope to the ceiling, called the sheriff, and hanged himself. He said, "Come and get me. I've killed all my family. I'll be dead time you get here."[60] Or, Kent asked, was it that he shot himself? On second thought, he does not remember, but, Kent says, Warren remembered the events. And Kent himself went to the house and saw the scene and the dead.[72]

In the poem the deaths of the Gillums are not so important as the reactions to the tragedy of the children in the school Warren attended. There may have been some children, Warren speculates on his remembering, whom the murderer was responsible for bringing to school. No children were murdered; Warren invented them. The impact on a sensitive mind of a

sensational event can be so great that it sometimes cannot dis-
tinguish embroidery from the bloody truth. In an interview we
talked about the poem.

FCW   Is the death of the Gillum family . . .

RPW   Actually a man killed his family, his whole family, when
I was in school, and with an ice pick and not only with an ice pick
but also with a hatchet. He killed a whole family and committed
suicide.

FCW   That was in Trenton?

RPW   No, that was in Guthrie. I've forgotten what the name was.
I've forgotten. I was in about the sixth grade. And the word came that
the father had killed the entire family. That was almost literally a
straight narrative. The trouble is most of the time it's not just the
narrative you're telling. It really is a character sketch or a bit of sym-
bolism, you see. That's the problem right there. It's to find the thing
that expands into something larger.[95]

Warren's memory of the wait for the children to come to school
may be a curious instance of a creative mind's remembering its
own invention as reality.

The county historian of Todd County (Mrs. Frances Marion
Williams) says that the killing of the Gillums happened around
Trenton, but that she left it out of her history. It was, she says,
"too grisly."[64] (Think how much of the world would be omitted
from the history books and from the understanding of man if
that were a valid working method for a historian. Indeed how
much would be omitted from poetry and from the Bible!) The
house still stands in Todd County, one of those human land-
marks stared at by the local people and pointed out as its own
kind of phenomenon. Mrs. Williams's father went to the scene
with the local coroner, and he often said that "that was the
absolutely worst sight he had ever seen."[84]

In such a violent crime the sudden change from daily life to
disaster may be revealed in images of the quick change from the
trivial to the terrible. The stark contrast is effective because of
the strange ironies. Warren's poem begins with the ordinariness, even the grossness, of the Gillums and of a day in a

small-town school. The destruction of the run-of-the-mill or even of the unattractive may seem as bad as the ruination of beauty. The Gillums "weren't so bright, or clean, or clever." (Compare Ransom's "Dead Boy," in which the deceased child was "not beautiful, nor good, nor clever.") "And their noses were sometimes imperfectly blown, / But they always got to school the weather whatever, / With old lard pail full of fried pie, smoked ham, and corn pone." The poetry of the country images and the uneducated desire for learning is based as truly on reality as sociology would like to be. The Gillum children are dutiful, at least on the elementary level. Theirs was the same search as that of Warren's father and his Grandfather Penn. The incongruity, the intensity of the search, and the tragedy of a family's death (already named in the title) are developed in the first stanza of the poem.

Five or six stanzas create a situation where the poet for the moment appears to be patronizing to these cartoon or comic-strip Southern backwoods stereotypes. All the images portray country appearance, character, personal disorder, and igno-rance. It is the country of the Old Southwest humorists, where "the whang-doodle whooped and the dang-whoodle snorted" (deleted after *Promises*). But the mood is established ironically, for the puzzles of existence are as complex and profound for the minds of people like the Gillums (in their terms) as they are for the deepest of philosophers. The poem, Cleanth Brooks has written, "strives to win the reader to the unsentimental com-passion that comes only when one has accepted the not very pretty facts."[106]

The intelligent but unlearned may indulge in philosophical speculations even when they have not learned the vocabularies. It is easy to foresee early in the poem the conclusion Old Slat Gillum will reach about his world. Slat is a talker, so much so that he stops passersby on the street to proclaim his views of the condition of man. "Say, mister," he says, with country formality refusing to use the name or the first name of someone he does not know very well. Perhaps the man he stops is even a stranger, and Slat cannot avoid a declaration of his personal belief—or disbelief.

"Say, mister,
I'll name you what's true fer folks, ever-one.
Human-man ain't much more'n a big blood blister,
    All red and proud-swole, but one good squeeze and he's gone."

Here and in subsequent stanzas, Slat Gillum declares the un-
warranted arrogance of man, "red and proud-swole," and his
actual triviality and pain, "a big blood blister"—a sore or injury
on the body of the world. But he also declares the duty of man
and a father: the obligation to provide education, Slat Gillum
swears, "so / they kin git they chance," he will "git 'em larned
before his own time came to die." So he sends them to school
to learn.

But one schoolday the Gillums do not appear. Finally word
comes, and Warren, in terms that emphasize the "tragic death"
(words in the title that echo the manner of a newspaper headline), names what each was doing when his turn came for Slat
Gillum's ice pick. In his hopeless meditations, Slat apparently
decided that the likeness between man and blood blister is so
great that even learning will not do any good (that is, however,
a point that Warren permits the reader to assume). Or perhaps
Slat came to the conclusion that for him and his family (and the
world) life did not present sufficient reward to endure its processes.

The poem concludes in the last four stanzas with the school
lesson (though not the one in the books) for the children who
knew the Gillum family. The classroom lives through the usual
routine of the day (scraping chalk, steaming windows, the landscape through the window), but the students meditate on the
Gillums, and their thoughts turn to things of the world as
insignificant as Old Slat's blood blister he always talked about.
"Which shoe, oh, which, was Brother putting on? / That was
something, it seemed, you just had to know. / But nobody
knew." Big lessons and little ones, the poem raises the question
of what may be learned from them. So all afternoon the children study the "arithmetic of losses," the abstract meaning of
death. But books do not provide the answers to questions about
some things, and even if they learned this one, *"There was*

another lesson, but we were too young to take up that one." But Slat
was not young. And he did take up the lesson. It is not an
exercise that education provides the answer for, either for those
in the poem or for the poet himself. Man may be more than a
blood blister; the poem does not itself say that he is not. Nor
does it say that he is. For the Gillums and the poet in these
poems, the search is as intense as that in the best lyrics of
Robert Frost, and as unrewarded. Perhaps even less rewarded.
Because Frost at the end of some of his poems, at least, could
be satisfied, or at least distracted, by getting back to earth for
a while. Warren could not. James Wright has written that the
poem is about "capricious horror" and that is therefore a "failure" because it has "no dramatic reason,"[116] but this reading
does not quite catch the significance of Old Slat's urgent statement when he, like Coleridge's wedding guest, stops a stranger
on the street to explain.[110] The poem is about horror, but it is
not a failure, because the horror is not capricious. So far as Old
Slat can tell, life is "capricious." When horror results because
one cannot tolerate his belief that all is capricious, the horror
itself is entirely explicable, but not capricious.

The same anonymity (or one might call it the general universality of the individual amid the minute particularity of images
in the setting) prevails in the poems about Mr. Moody and the
Gillums and in "Ballad: Between the Boxcars (1923)." Mr.
Moody is defined by what he quietly does, his work, and his
constant reading in the Bible, not by what he thinks; the poet
tells what kind of people the Gillums are and how the kids look
when they come to school; and we know the seriousness and
the wide prevalence of Old Slat's question. But the individuali-
ties of the wife and the children remain unknown. In the
tragedy of the boy who died between the boxcars, the poet
"can't even remember the name of the one who fell / Flat on his
ass, on the cinders, between the boxcars." This ballad has a
setting particularly characteristic of Guthrie, a very small town
but also an important railroad center. In Warren's youth a railroad was something to wonder at as well as a monster to play
with. For Thomas Wolfe a train was a great and marvelous link
to bring things from the outside world and, more important, at

least to the child, to carry the person to the world. The train seldom impinged so much on Warren's imagination. When it did, it was an instrument that helped the poet to reach for a larger meaning.

Most people of Guthrie half a century later are not much more certain of the name of the boy who died between the boxcars than Warren was. The tragedy comes because a boy was playing around a train, not escaping the place of his early life. How many boys may have fallen beneath a train in Guthrie no one knows, and no one, especially not the railroad, has published records. Particularity is not the point. Indeed, it is likely that no small town with a lot of trains has avoided some kind of tragedy between the boxcars. The date after the title of the poem, 1923, perhaps provides a clue, but it has not led me to an answer. (Warren actually wrote the first few lines in Rome, he says, in 1958).

Warren says the poem had "several sources. It is a common event, you might say. . . . It is not tied to anyone. It was part of that world."[95] Kent Greenfield remembers that one boy who died between the boxcars was named Larry Grizzard. At the time Kent was about twenty or twenty-five, and he is certain that Warren would have heard of the incident and remembered it. Mrs. Evelyn Hooser, one of Warren's teachers, even "would dare say" that 1923 was "sorta right." Jim Pendleton, an elder in the church, and his wife, Jenny Webb Pendleton, had four children.[73] One boy who fell and lost his life between the boxcars was the Pendletons' only son, over fifteen years old when he was killed. Boys like to play when freight trains were moving in the switchyard, to move from car to car. And the Pendleton boy, or whover it was who fell, failed to catch the ladder of the car and fell beneath its wheels, or those of the one behind it: "One more thing I remember perfectly well, / You go for the grip at the front, not the back, of the boxcars." Throughout the first part ("I Can't Even Remember the Name"), Warren uses the pronoun *you,* which he adopts with more frequency and accomplishment in fiction and poetry than any other writer I know. Whether or not the teller of the poetic tale heard the yell of the boy, "I remember its shape on his mouth, between the boxcars, / And it was shape that yours would be too if you fell / Flat on your ass, on the cinders, between the boxcars." And, perhaps, he suggests, if you fall on your ass in *any* of the riding or the activities of the world.

The first twenty-three lines of the second part of the poem ("He Was Formidable") create the imaginary future of the boy, not his death. For his age he was a baseball player with the skill of Kent Greenfield, and he was also skilled already as a lover. So the poet can imagine a tabloid headline, *"Woman Slays Self for His Love."* But one line after the account of his skill as a batter, there is the reminder that he "got spiked between the boxcars," and the line that ends the stanza on his capabilities as a lover recalls that he "spilled, as boys may, too soon, between the boxcars." Or, in the third stanza, there is another possibility: "he might have been boss of the best supermarket in town."

Part 2 asks questions that might be asked about the other characters in these poetic vignettes: "what is success, or failure, at the last?" Why also, the poet asks, "should we grieve for the name that boy might have made. . . ?" The stanza ends with a rather obscure question about the fate of us all. All fall between the boxcars. All have prayed that when the time comes, "we may know the poor self not alone, but with all" who come to the universal end, however it comes. Small consolation, to know that all must die and to know that death, regardless of its manner, always is a violent end. However it comes, it is "that clobber and slobber and grunt, between the boxcars." At the ultimate moment, everyone dies as a boy between the boxcars, and everyone can have consolation, small as it is, that he is not the only one who falls.

In the original volume of *You, Emperors, and Others,* the poem included a third part, more lyrical than narrative, with three stanzas about the boy who has died and his condition or status after death from various perspectives, and a fourth stanza is written on how "we live in the world." In *Selected Poems*, for better and for worse, Warren deleted the entire third part of the poem. Part 3 moves, as Warren often does, from stark event to momentous meaning. Four parallel stanzas progress from the

instant death of the boy to the conditions of living for all and
what is thought (usually nothing can be done) about them.
Three beautiful similes in the first stanza echo images that
might be used for the instant change from body to soul:

> He has fled like electricity down the telegraph wires into
>   prairies of distance where the single bird
>   sits small and black against the saffron sky,
>   and is itself.

And he has also fled like a glint of light on wet rails and like
a wild goose, unheard even by one who broods over how far
away the farthest railroad runs to the north.

After flight, the poem turns to the conditions of the remains
of death, the boy's by implication and death in general as revealed in extremely specific images: "cold chemical combus-
tion," "the acrid sap of red oak," and "the delectable
crystallization of sugar in grape jelly." The third stanza of Part
3 contains three parallel abstract and philosophical statements
about the boy and what his death has shown about death. He
has "profounded a theorem," "broken past atmospheres" to
"revelation," and "explored a calculus of your unexpected
probabilities, / and what now *is* was never probable, / but only
is." The last stanza projects the boy's death even to further
abstractions, and now the "we," that is, everyone alive, is, or
are, associated with the boy in his mortality. We live in the
world, and we do not like it because of things like the death of
the boy between the boxcars. Consequently, we do "all we can
to reject it utterly" and even, the poem says, to reject the memory of the death of the boy, but we cannot. This "recollection,"
the poet says at the end of the poem, he would like to "eject,"
get it out of his mind, perhaps by writing about it. Not able to
"eject" it, the poet can only wish to "reject" it, to deny that the
story of the fall between the boxcars and the resultant death
ever existed, "but cannot." The poem ends, then, with the poet
staring his own death squarely in the eye.

As "Ballad: Between the Boxcars" at the end of the poem
shows the long-lasting effect on the adult persona of a tragic

event that befell a boy beneath a train in the railroad town, "Recollections in Upper Ontario, from Long Before" (1980) begins with the lingering effect in the mind of the persona of a terrible tragedy that came to an elderly couple also beneath a train in a railroad town. It is "later by years" and "a thousand miles north, on the Hudson Bay slope," but the rememberer still wakes up at night and ponders what he does not know. A loon laughs at the bird's own joke, and the speaker wonders "if it is on me. / That is, if mine could be called one." Always it is a locomotive that wakes him to his dream, though there is no track within three hundred miles. The fear of the coming of the train-dream or of the owl asking "who—*who-who*" wakes his conscience and the guilt of his knowledge dominates the first four stanzas before Warren gets to the causative event. Actually, it is not the guilt of the living person in the poem but his memory of an event no one, perhaps not even the primary participants, understands or ever understood.

Few poems in the entire Warren canon present such a confusion of event and of feelings as this poem about memories recalled in upper Ontario. The story from the railroad town—perhaps Guthrie—begins with the end of things and then flashes back to the beginning, the marriage of Zack and his Mag. The poem recalls Zack's bedding of Mag (as imagined by the poet). She had a club foot,

> and Zack and his Mag, young now,
> Getting ready for bed, them maybe just married.
> Saw how she was trying to get off her gear and not show
> That foot. Yes, there in my head, I saw it, and saw
> How he took it, the foot. Leaned over and kissed it.
>
> And tears gone bright in her eyes.

The foot is as indicative of the identity of Mag as Billie Potts's birthmark is the seal of his, and it is to take part in her fate more even than the birthmark did in that poem. The narrator continues, "But all the years later I'd only see / How he'd try not to see it. Then / Blow out the lamp." In summer Zack stares after he goes to bed; in winter he watches the shadows east by the firelight. Before he can make love to Mag now he has to "handle himself."

Zack and Mag became old and remained poor, and they had to "scrounge coal off the L & N tracks." Mag helps, "face knobby, eyes bleared, / Mouth dribbling with snuff, skirts swinging / Above the old brogan she's fixed for her clubfoot." Once when a train comes it looks as if Mag's brogan gets "caught / In a switch-V." And the narrator watches as Zack tries to pull her free from the track and from the path of the train. For a second it looks as if she gets free

> standing,
> Then down—now over both rails—
> Down for good, and the last
> Thing I see is his hands out. To grab her, I reckoned.

Simple and plain as the tragedy appears to be, that is the moment of confusion and meaning to be faced forever after by Zack and the watching boy and the poet.

The corpse is carried away ("hamburger now"), the boy flees, and the coroner comes and rules that it is " 'An accident.' "

After the burial in the rain, to which few came, the boy meets Zack drunk on the street, defending himself, accusing the boy.

> "Yeah, you come spyen on me!
> Down thar in the ditch, in them weeds. Well, you're wrong!"
>
> . . . .
> "I ne'er tetched her! She fell. Nigh got myself kilt
> Count of her durn shoe!" Then he,
> Old fingers like rusty nails in my biceps: "Stuck up!
> You durn little butterfly ketcher—but got enough sense
> To haul-ass afore the durn coroner come."

Exonerated, Zack is now implicated only by his assertions of an innocence never denied by the law. Probably it is not that he is defending himself because he is drunk, but that he is drunk because of a grief otherwise not even implied, or because he did not try enough to save her (perhaps even tried to wedge her foot), or because he has not had the strength to face his crisis and tragedy. The boy listens, "And something inside me, it grew."

And it is still growing in the far north on the canoe trip when he wakes to the old dream and the "brass-bound express / Comes boiling over the hill, whistle crazy." The joys of the northwoods are paradisiacal. Dawn is "a riot of glory." Breakfast comes tasty from the cookfire. The canoes "glide out . . . on the unrippling sheen / Of day's silver and gold. . . ."

> A voice is singing its joy—and is this
> The same world I stood in,
> In the ditch, years ago,
> And saw what I saw?
>
> Or what did I see?

Now it is daytime, and he does not know. Last night he had the dream because he did not know, and tonight the dream will recur. The coroner did not know. And Zack did not. And no one knows what he saw or what Zack did not or could not do. The events of the poem are as complex and as unresolvable as those in any fiction or poem ever created—in *All the King's Men* or any of the critical or poetic puzzlings of the poet. And that is the power of the poem. (Frankly, it kept me awake too, last night.) Neither poor old Zack's whiskey nor all the puzzlings of narrators and readers will ever know what Zack did.

In *Tale of Time: Poems 1960-1966* the title poem of the volume turns again to the Warren family in Guthrie, especially to the death (and life) of the poet's mother, as "Mortmain" in *Emperors* recalls the father. Within "Tale of Time"one remarkable study is the vignette of the insane druggist. The most substantial poem about the times and the people of the poet's childhood, however, is a nine-page (in the original volumn) and five-part poem called "The Day Dr. Knox Did It."

This is one of Warren's most extended and substantial Guthrie or Cerulean poems. It is based on an incident that gave Warren much to think about in his early teens. In the poet's late career the poem is a rendering of responses to actual circumstances in his early life. On the other hand, parts of the poem that seem to be factual may be altogether from the realm of the imagination. But the poem, as Warren says in another context, is real. "The world is real. It is there."

Like something with the characteristics of a memory and a diary, "The Day Dr. Knox Did It" begins with an atmosphere that has become almost traditional in the South for writings about disaster, violent death, and lynching. At first, maturity and a modern perspective seem to dominate the attitude toward the rural community, and it has already begun to look like the dead towns in contemporary depopulated areas of the South. Cerulean Springs, where the boy persona is visiting, is

> only a piece of country road
> mislaid, somehow, among the white houses,
>
> as the houses, too, had got mislaid
> among the last big oaks and big tulip trees left
> from the old forest-time.

Heat, white dust, and blazing light remain always in the memory of the poet, who recalls August, 1914, in the ninety-five-degree heat at three in the afternoon. A nine-year-old boy moves toward the coolness of a stream, but hears a sound. Although the poem does not name it, the sound was a shot, and Warren himself actually heard it when he was eleven years old.

What the shot is like is described in Part II—one board falling loud and flat on another. Still not naming the suicide, he tells factually about a man's climbing to a barn loft "to arrange himself." Through the memory of the child, the mature narrator contrasts boyhood and the self-inflicted death of an adult. The consciousness of the boy tries to penetrate the older despairing mind. "How long had he lain, just looking?" The phrase "just looking" is as uncommunicative as "did it." The central event is not yet the suicide. Indeed, that is never the point. The poem is about the immediate and later the lasting effect on the boy. Nothing reports the information that would be in a newspaper or in the vital statistics. Details are of the place, the things that impinge on the mind of the boy. The poetry is not primarily what *was* in the mind of the poet when he *was* a boy learning of the suicide. The point *is* the meditation of the poet as he thinks now of a suicide he encountered and reacted to more than half a century before.

Dr. Sterling Price Quisenberry, a dentist of Cerulean Springs and a native of Winchester, Kentucky, climbed into the barn loft (as in the poem) of Dr. White and, as a local newspaper reported, "shot himself with a pistol," "leaving no explanation for the deed"—as the poem itself leaves no explanation. Thirty-two years old, he left a wife and two small children, a girl and a boy (*Winchester Democrat* 16 June 1916). Warren never knew the doctor; the things of most consequence to the young poet-to-be were that he actually heard the death-shot and that he was left with immediate speculations about the event and its meanings as well as meditations for years on the human implications of such an act. Never in the poem is there an indication of the hint given in a newspaper that "financial troubles" might have been a cause (*Hopkinsville Kentuckian* 15 June 1916). To assign a cause in the poem would be to narrow the range of the possibilities.

The poem is a study of the man thinking of the boy thinking of the thinking of the man preparing for suicide. Twice the poem asks "*how long* [italics mine] he had lain there." Not even what he was thinking. But what does the length of time that he lay there show? Uncertainty or indecision? The length of his pain? The nature of desperate and painful indecision? Warren does not provide an answer and does not expect the reader to find one. What he expects to provoke is meditation, like that of the narrator. Really, also, despite the youth of the boy, the question is not limited to him, and the answer is no different for boy or man. Age—whether youthful or mature—does not bring one closer to knowledge.

The perspective of childhood dominates the third part. Under the cedar trees that are like those of the old Penn place outside Cerulean, the boy turns to the wisdom of age for the answer and asks directly in the first line, " 'But why did he do it, Grandpa?' I said." Again, as in Part II, he remembers that Dr. Knox arranged himself. The arranging, with the repetition, assumes a new importance. It shows the planning, the extended deliberateness of the decision to commit suicide, definitely, neatly. Neatly, perhaps, in search of as much order as a suicidal mind can attain. Also, out of concern for those who will find the body.

Grandpa's answers are not meaningful to the boy. He can reply only that "It's one of those things," and the disastrous things of life like this are never known. When the boy declares that there must be a reason (perhaps even the doctor who committed suicide did not know it), all that Grandpa can say is that folks "up and die." There may be no reasons to be known by man. Some mystery brings death into the world and all our woe. The word *die* forces the old man back to his memories of the varieties of death in the Civil War, but again he ends without an answer. "The words, they stopped. / . . . The eyes looked away." From his search through the war and his desire for meaning, he concludes that death does not have to be particularly meaningful. Anybody can do what Dr. Knox did. Indeed, it is something "any fool can do."

But again the boy asks for a reason.

At last the question has been driven home to Grandpa, the elder, the old Confederate veteran, the adult such as the poet-boy has become years afterward when he recalls the episode. In its immediacy, the question is why a man, Dr. Knox, *chose* to die, to kill himself. The answer comes in generalities: "For some folks the world gets too much." The answer is so impersonal that the poet speaks of the tongue, "it said." That statement takes no mind, or at least very little: nothing explains the nature of the world in general or the conditions for the doctor when he made the decision. And how does it get "too much"? For a man or for the doctor? Through three parts of the poem Warren has created great impact by merely describing the place where a suicide happens, the sound the gun made, and the questions in the mind of a child younger than the dead man and that of a man much older than either. Part III ends when Grandpa says, "For some folks. . . ." Not for all. That is to say, suicide is optional. Some folks may decide to do it, and some may not. Or, perhaps, the conditions of the world are variable. Some folks may live in a circumstance where suicide seems necessary, and some may not. Neither Grandpa nor the poet chooses between the alternatives of decisions and of conditions in the world.

Talking with Grandpa does not end the troubling of the boy. Who is to say, in the first place, whether the focus of the poem is on the troubling of a boy about the meaning of death and suicide or whether it is on the puzzling of the mature poet? The environment, the event, and the grandparent have been created and characterized with infinite care, and only the thoughts of the boy have been reported. The poem is not a story but a meditation. At any rate, "ten days after the event"—*ten* days—the boy goes to the loft with the son of the man who committed suicide—yes, the son, and he too has been meditating on his own father's choice, and the meaning of the decision. This incident is poetic creation based on imagination. Warren did not know the dentist's son or that he had a son.[95] The persona does not know why they go to the place, and so far as is reported, the son himself does not know: "He just said, 'Come on.' . . ." In this way, also, the world does not provide answers. Part IV reports the response to those who visit the scene of death afterward. He had expected "an awful mess," but "the place looked clean." The boy wonders only about "who had cleaned up the mess." For the moment, he seems to have forgotten all else, not only why the man killed himself, but all the other things that followed in the wake of suicide and what came before and during and after.

Thus ends the story of the man who climbed to the loft and put the muzzle of the shotgun in his mouth. The change from an ax to an ice pick in the deaths of the Gillum family is a strong and ironic contrast to the change from a neat pistol hole to a bloody shotgun splattering in the poem about the death of Dr. Knox. Somehow the instruments of death seem poetically appropriate—small but neat wounds in a mass murder and a massive bleeding in a single suicide. Left with no answer given even by the grandfather, or the son of the dead man, the boy flees, "wondering." And wondering is all that any of them or anyone else may do. The boy lies in a stream as water flows over him, and here he attains the only and ultimate recognition: "like water, the world / would flow, flow away, on forever."

Subsequent events or incidents in much later years provide only more wondering, no more enlightenment. Once in San Francisco years later fog blotted out all but the boy become man and the goat droppings on which he stood on Telegraph Hill. Then his "heart, in a rage like joy, / burst." It was a rage, and it was not joy. Perhaps it is like the rage or the despair of whatever emotion Dr. Knox had. The persona knows only that his heart burst. Still he does not know why, neither the condition on the outside that caused it nor the emotion on the inside that resulted. At another moment of recollection he made love to a girl by another sea (not the Pacific), and, despite tears, he cannot "remember her face." Their lovemaking and the emotions it involved were or have become as unknown as the motive of Dr. Knox. Not to remember the face in Warren is not to know the person.

At the end the persona recalls his sins and weaknesses. Changing to that universal second person Warren so often uses, *you,* the persona reminds all that everyone, "like you, [is] the perfect image." Of the creator? Or what creator? Or what creation? He remembers that when he fled toward the sound, toward Dr. Knox, he also fled toward himself, and, we may assume, toward us. Despairingly, the poem says, "there is / no water to wash the world away." In the terms of the world, there is no baptism, no washing away, such as the boy lying in the stream wished to experience. And the terms are the world's; they are not sins. There may be no sins to be washed away; at least the poem does not say there are any.

Surprisingly, at the end we are told that "we must frame . . . more firmly the idea of good." But the poem provides no materials from which to frame that notion or concept. It only asserts that somewhere or somehow they exist. But the need for them continues, and the poet ends with the need. Writing the poem, years after Dr. Knox did it, he hears his young daughter weeping in the next room for her dog who has "been killed on the road." In general terms, the dog has died as Dr. Knox died, and the poet is no more able to provide an answer for the girl than Grandpa did for the boy. The poem essentially is a powerfully emotional treatment of the need for answers that do not exist.

The title, "The Day Dr. Knox Did It," remains as puzzling as the motives of Dr. Knox. Three parts are about the day, and two are about the short-term and the long-term future of the boy and the effect of the day on him. Truly, the title does not cover the subject. Symbolically, perhaps (and who can say more?), the day is the moment of awakening to the realities and the meaning—better, the lack of stated meaning—of life. As such, it is the day that defines all of life—or fails to define it. The inadequacy of the title suggests the failure of everything to answer. The day begins with the boy's first "Why?" and extends even beyond the poem.

The suicide of the doctor is not the point. In spite of all the minutely described particularities of Cerulean Springs, the unique character of Grandpa, the details of the way Dr. Knox did it, and the images that make the poem poetry, the point is the universality of the meaning. By some mysterious alchemy the real and the imagined concrete details form the art and flow together with the meaning to become beautiful, perplexing, and profound poetry. Cerulean Springs and Grandpa as they are in history and in the memory of Robert Penn Warren (in his talk about them) seem to be so exactly themselves that one expects Dr. Knox, the boy, his son, and the event to be exactly themselves too, even though Warren did not know them personally —only the sound of the gunshot. And they are. But they represent also life and the way it all is. As Grandpa says, " 'Folks— yes, folks, they up and die.' / 'But, Grandpa—' I said. And he: 'They die.' " Thank about it as long as "you," or "we," may, that is all we can know. The limitations of knowledge do not diminish the impact on the heart.

For some reason Dr. Knox determines to bring an end to his speculations.

In "Orphanage Boy" in *Now and Then* Warren also returns to the time and scene of his early childhood. The people and events could be those of any Southern farm before the advent of modern ways. The character told about, Al, comes from the orphanage to earn his keep and work his way to maturity, perhaps as a young apprentice once came to the farm of Gabriel Thomas Penn in the old days in Cerulean Springs. The perva-

sive poverty of the rural South—even on the better farms—
prevails, and Al would be "what you'd call / Hired boy if he got
enough to / Call hire." While chopping wood, he teaches the
speaker "all the / Dirty words I'd never heard of." He explains
fun on the farm too in a subtle suggestion of early sexual
experiences and sodomy with the animals.

Al is more sensitive, however, than he seems to be in the first
stanza, and something goes on in his head besides vulgarity and
obscenity. He even has a streak of poetry in his spirit. At the
end of the day he sits on the stile "with / Bob, the big white
farm bulldog," and watches the sun set or the moon come up.
But the pastoral life ends when a copperhead bites Bob.

> Just after
> Supper one night my uncle stood
> On the front porch and handed a
> Twelve-gauge to Al, and said, "Be sure
> You do it right back of the head."
> He never named Bob's name.

Al's knowledge of the dirty words is no cure or cover for the
tenderness of his heart. He takes the gun, goes with the narrator
to the woods, shoots his canine friend, hands the gun to his
other friend, and says, "Git away, you son-a-bitch." He lies
down on the leaves, cries, and disappears during the night. Six
months later the teller of the story discovers that Al made a real
grave for Bob and put a wooden cross on it. The one-line last
stanza meditates on the effort expended in making the grave:
"It must have taken nigh moonset."

This short poem is as objective and noncommittal and stark
as anything in Hemingway or any other work by Warren. It is
like a fable or a parable, but it is too homely, too rich in detail,
too specific to be one of those forms. It is Al and Bob, not a
certain rich man in the Bible or an envious frog in Aesop. If the
poem, like Emily Dickinson's goblin bee, does not state its sting,
it nevertheless has one—or a great many. It is a poem of numerous afterthoughts, many of them possible, none of them prova-
ble beyond dispute from the text itself. The conditions it

reflects may be attributable to a Southern or rural way of life, man's theological condition, the haphazard luck of the world, or the status of man—or dog. It is a world of parentless children, snake-bitten bogs, hard work, pain, thoughtful meditation by the outwardly callous, exchange between dog and boy like some of the exchanges between different kinds of creatures in a poem by James Dickey, the necessity of using death to put a creature out of a pain worse than death, the duty of the lowly to put the still lowlier out of pain. Perhaps one may not be able to face the world. Al runs away from what he has seen and what he has had to do. He curses; he knows the dirty world. But he forms a friendship with Bob, and he is able to kill him when it becomes necessary. Al's crass exterior melts, and he weeps. Then in the darkness he tries to give a fellow creature a proper burial, and he does not wait to proclaim the ceremoniousness of the night burial. The meanings of the poem may be numerous, but they are presented in one of Warren's simplest vehicles.

"Orphanage Boy" and the burial, Warren says, represent almost factually a situation that Warren had known.[95] The point is not the use of reality or the varieties of meanings or even the certainty or uncertainty about the condition of creatures in the world. The accomplishment of the poem is that it sets in motion a chain of unforgettable ponderables without choosing at all between them. Always Warren contemplates the mysteries; sometimes he ponders on many of them in his writing; this time he leaves them altogether to the reader to interpret for himself.

Stories of deaths and of funerals and other death customs and rituals play a major role in Southern life, the talk of a traditional society, and literature about folk peoples. A good many of Warren's poems deal with death and funerals, not in what some critics would call an emphasis on death, but simply as a part of life. (It seems to be the custom for an urban or a sophisticated society to turn to morticians and perhaps mentally to cancel death out of the ways of the living.) One who is aware of death and dying may be simply one who is aware of all the processes of existence.

Two death poems that most resemble each other in Warren are "Boy Wandering in Simms' Valley" (1977) and a poem in the volume *Being Here:* "Filling Night with the Name: Funeral as Local Color" (1979). The poems have in common the death of a wife, the survival of the husband, the response of the husband to the death, the importance of the presence or absence of neighbors, the consequences of the death, the loneliness of the survivor. But the poems are also contrasting in that one ("Filling Night") has a community and the other does not; one responds to the death and the loneliness with strength, the other with suicide; one is a community affair, the other is absolutely solitary.

The death and the funeral of "Filling Night with the Name" are as elemental as the earth itself. "It was all predictable," the poem begins. The dead wife has a name unpleasant in meaning and even in sound, "Mrs. Clinch." The corpse lies

> gut-rigid there
> In the coffin, withered cheeks subtly rouged, hair
> Frizzled and tinted, with other marks of skill
> Of the undertaker. . . .

The images are so stark and earthy in the true rural fashion that one wonders what Mr. Clinch might have seen in his wife. But to him she was a person and a mate.

The neighbors do what neighbors can to ease the sorrow. They offer to stay with Mr. Clinch during the night after the funeral and to cook his food. But he replies "When a thing's gonna be . . . git used to it fast." So he wipes away a tear and goes to his farm. Though he is not hungry and does not eat, he tends to his duty. He milks the cow, even in his good clothes.

He cannot go to bed, cannot go to the bed "of / Starched sheets by some kindly anonymous hand pulled tight." He starts to write his son who was for some reason too far away to come to the funeral,

> But no word would come, and sorrow and joy
> All seemed one—just the single, simple word *whip-o-will.*

> For the bird was filling the night with the name: *whip-o-will.*

For me, the conclusion of the poem defies the intellect, though not the feelings. Warren says he chose a spelling not given by the dictionaries to represent more accurately the sound of the bird than the spelling *whippoorwill* does. The bird fills the night with the sound of its own name, and anyone who has heard a whippoorwill (few there be who have ever seen one except remotely in the day sky) knows that it is a sound as remarkable as that of the mourning dove and as mysterious as the calls of any number of species of owls. But the night is filled with the sound of the bird, and the head of the grieving husband is also filled with the eerie night-sound. Warren has created the intensity of his emotions and communicated to the reader that intensity and something of the grief and the mystery, but he has not communicated the rational idea of what it is that is filling the night and the husband's head, and I suggest that he does not wish to do so. One may no more know the meaning of the cry of the bird than he may know the fullness of the meaning of death and of the obligation of those who must live on alone in their grief and solitude. All, as the preacher says, is shrouded in mystery; and to dig too deep into the mystery might be a little like exploring the grave of the dead.

The spirit and the fidelity of one of the characters in "Boy Wandering in Simms' Valley" is warm, almost a bright glow. Solitude, sickness, death, violence, suicide in the last stanza (this time one line), and a conclusion speculating on the ultimate meanings of this episode and all reality—ingredients common in Warren's poems are here. But in Simms' valley there has also been an extraordinary strength. The persona wanders into a solitary valley, where Simms for long years "had nursed a wife till she died." Before her death they lived without kin or visitors. When she dies Simms lies down by his wife, takes his shotgun as Dr. Knox did, and shoots himself. But the place is so isolated that no one discovers the bodies, or what remains of them, for two years.

Years after that "I came," and the boy found desolation at least as bleak as that in Robert Frost's "The Black Cottage." The ruin is so extensive that no one offers to buy the house at "tax-sale." Sheets, blankets, windows, the house itself—all is decay but one object. The last image the boy sees is of "the old

enameled bedpan, high on a shelf." It suggests human waste or
filth, helplessness, pain, and deathbed sickness. But the implications contradict the factual object. The bedpan proves the
care of one person for another, care even for the bedpan that
is left "high on a shelf" even after the sick one died, a love that
endures and survives all mortal ills and obligations—all the
material devastation. So in the final lines of the poem and the
last glimpse at the scene, the despicable bedpan becomes the
subject of the boy's reverie. At the moment, "the last sun fell
on me." So he stands "wondering what life is, and love, and
what they may be." That is, I believe, "what they may be" in
terms of one person's great and dedicated love for another.
"Boy Wandering in Simms' Valley" (with the pun in the title)
speculates on the infinite capacities of the human heart, not
on the unanswerable questions about God and man in the
vast spaces of the universe. It is a different kind of considera-
tion of the eternal speculations about what man is. There is almost no greater devastation, or isolation, than that of Simms
and his wife in their last years and of their place after their
death. But even though Warren may still puzzle about the
infinities, human love may be beyond the highest calculations
of man—all revealed in a thing so lowly as a well-preserved
bedpan.

My hunch that Simms and his ailing wife were old citizens
of Todd County was wrong. In January, 1979, Warren told me
that he did find the cabin that was a source for the poem, but
it was (and perhaps is) located in a backwoods area in Vermont,
hundreds of miles from the places I had expected it to be and
years from the period of Warren's life when I thought he had
seen it. The images, the scene, and the people are concrete, but
nothing identifies them as being New England Yankees or Todd
County citizens in Kentucky. The treatment of setting is a good
indication of something about the ways of Warren's imagination and of all good poets. The older Warren places himself in
the mind of a boy, and he finds two cultures with enough in
common so that he can write from what he has seen in one and
yet include nothing that violates the life or the spirit of the
other. Narrative, love, and poetry transcend as always whatever

limitations may seem to be imposed upon them by region and place and time.

Old Memories

Warren's poems are altogether rooted in the living, breathing, hurting, and often bleeding sources of the people, the episodes, and the places he has known. The images, tone, atmosphere, dialect, people—the whole world of southern rural Kentucky— are rendered as exactly as the worlds of Welty, Porter, Wolfe, Faulkner, and the best Southern writers. In his poetry Warren is as exact as any of them, but, naturally, as poetry, not as documentary. Most of the fiction is a different matter. Usually it is set in the South, but away from the worlds of Guthrie and Cerulean that Warren had known when he went to Vanderbilt. But a great number of his poems are set precisely in those two places.

"Old Flame" recalls a forgotten love dream, which begins in youthful silence and ends with a spoken encounter that modifies but does not end the dreams of youth. "Evening Hour" succeeds in recapturing youth for a fleeting moment but depicts the failure of the youth in attempting to recover memories of his parents and his heritage. "Amazing Grace" turns from youthful and country religion to the perpetual puzzlements of life thereafter. "Orphanage Boy" is an account of tenderness in a boy who superficially appears to be a hoodlum and a master of obscenities. Collectively, these poems represent youth, first as it is lived, and second and more meaningfully, as it has been lived and can be recalled with knowledge and a bit of nostalgia. Part I of *Now and Then* is not only somewhat different from Warren's earlier turnings back to his past, but it is also a unified collection of poems with a scheme of their own.

"Old Flame" (1978) catches the desire and the frustration of childhood romance, the forgetfulness that follows, and the way that old age contemplates the long-ago in the relic of the once-provocative beloved. Perhaps the frequency of such a relationship, the simplicity of the emotions, and the mixture of wonder and the commonplace are reflected in the iambic quatrains with

an abab rhyme scheme. Images of the poem are reminiscent of
the young wonder of Faulkner's Isaac McCaslin about his bride
and the partly planned enticements of the young woman. The
mysteries of sexuality are barely camouflaged when the first
stanza describes the "sausage-like trotters" that "toted incom-
parable glory down the street." The feelings of the admirer of
Herrick's Julia certainly do not surpass those of Warren's boy,
who marvels at the revelation and the concealment of the
maiden's charms. Her "twin braids" move with "a bewitching
twitch," and the youth does not have to be told that a great deal
is moving besides the braids. So for nine years (in the ways of
youth) "no word ever passed," and thus ends the youthful
affair. Three stanzas create this first glory, and three end it.
Returned home, a stranger, the old man hears his name called
out by "a grisly old dame" (by stark contrast, in the day of her
glory, she spoke never a word), a dame with "gingham, false
teeth, gray hair." Recognizing that "pile of age-litter," hearing
"at last conversation," he learns that she is a widow, a grandmother, "comfortably fixed."

The images of the last stanza suggest how time grinds on
until the black Cadillacs of the last procession "scarcely hold a
funereal pace." Sometimes the reminiscer forgets the name of
the girl, but he can usually remember the legs and the braids.
But he says nothing of the glory that once the legs "toted." At
the first and the last of the poem and of life, the one who recalls
does not know enough. The poem ends with his saying he
remembers "never, never a face." The lusts of youth and the
passing years never made the young man know the woman as
a face, a person, an identity. Only the glory of youth, the
possibility of wonder and love. The meaning of the poem is a
commonplace; it represents the disappointment of anyone who
has ever admired beauty and then witnessed its vanquishment
by years. "Old Flame" actually is an account of the ultimate
doom of dreamers or lovers who, unlike those on Keats's urn,
live on and come to knowledge.

"Evening Hour" (1978) is also a recollection of a childhood
village, with the narrator placing himself in the graveyard. A
boy hunting arrowheads there almost unthinkingly looks for

the flints and glances "up at a buzzard's high sun-glinting wings, / Not thinking of flesh and its nature"—even in a grave-yard. When a freight train strives with its load, the boy pauses "for maybe two minutes," but then he lingers until it is so late that the lights come on in the town. The narrator of the poem recollects the boy, whose relationship to himself, though prob-ably close, is never defined. The teller of the poem does know that the boy felt "the crazy impulse grow / To lay ear to earth for what voices beneath might say."

Two poems, "Walk by Moonlight in Small Town" and "Eve-ning Hour," are meditations with identifiable Guthrie settings that are important to the meaning. The walk (from *Promises)* passes by stores on "Main Street"—the same kind of street as the one in Guthrie, but with a different name—past boxcars one would see in a railroad town. The walker crosses the track and mounts the hill to the school, as Warren did as a child. Almost as in Emily Dickinson's "Because I Could Not Stop for Death," he sees children playing "with no sound," but the children stop in his fantasy and watch him. Again the poem ends with philo-sophical speculation:

> Might a man but know his Truth, and might
> He live so that life, by moon or sun,
> In dusk or dawn, would be all one—
> Then never on a summer night
> Need he stand and shake in that cold blaze of Platonic light.

Warren is not like any other major Southern writer in the use that he makes of the world of his origins. Faulkner usually creates a profound and meaningful narrative that concludes spectacularly, humorously, ironically, or with an abrupt twist or confrontation. Wolfe arrives at a lyrical and emotional sum-mation about his hero or his hero's views. Eudora Welty leaves the reader with a puzzle that continues unraveling far beyond the literal end of the story. But Warren ends, more than anyone else, with philosophical and religious speculation about the meaning of what he has done and the place of man in the world. Almost every one of the poems based on Guthrie and

Cerulean ends with speculations that would be bad poetry if
they were rendered in the manner of a lesser poet—even as in
the lesser poems of Frost. But they do not end didactically or
in a pedagogical tone. What saves them is unanswered speculation, puzzlement beyond rational thought. It is hard to be abstract and philosophical as Warren is in his poetry, and it takes
a talent as great as his or Melville's to follow that route.

If Frost is best when he is indirect and if Warren is seldom
so indirect as Frost is at his best, Warren is a better philosophical poet than Frost. He does not provide an answer or preach.
He makes a philosophical statement that creates a lyrical and
emotional response to the mortal condition both in readers who
sympathize with Warren's questioning and in those who may
for the moment suspend their belief and share the poet's yearning. Despite the influence of Eliot on Warren and the other
Fugitives, Warren practices a poetry that openly reveals the
emotions and philosophy and personality of the poet. Like Melville in *Moby-Dick* and like the Bible in style if not in faith,
Warren reveals a poetry of meaning. More than any other great
poet of the twentieth century, he is able to derive a stated
meaning from his stories and his images. Warren is like a
prophet who has lost his faith but retained his need and his
fervor.

Again and again, when Warren is asked about his belief in
God, he has said that he is a naturalist, but always he adds
quickly that he is a "great yearner"—a yearner for a belief and
a yearner for a God. A critic should hesitate and tremble before
disagreement with such a firm and stark statement by the author, but in most senses of the word Warren is not a naturalist.
Of course no one is utterly a naturalist. The most unqualified
statements of despair and naturalism that I know come in places
in the work of Theodore Dreiser, yet in other places his characters act altogether in contradiction to the theoretical statements
of naturalism. In the American literature anthology that Warren
helped to compile and edit, one aspect of what is called the
"paradox in literary naturalism" is the belief that "all behavior
is dictated by the laws of nature."[33] That is to say, everything
of the body, the mind, and what is called the heart is deter-

mined by environment, heredity, chemistry (Dreiser's "chem-isms"). If anyone believes that, certainly no author can practice the belief. It is apparent in Warren's own works that he is not entitled to claim merely and simply the title "naturalist." He seems to be using it, when he says it, as the opposite of "super-naturalist." On the human level, the relative but high degree of freedom in making decisions that his characters have, the willed evil of some characters, and the obstinate heroism of some characters are proof enough that Warren believes too much in the freedom and the potentiality of man to be the naturalist he claims to be. The uncertainties of his sometimes open and sometimes concealed speculations, added to his Melvillean de-spairs and yearnings, are the basis of a poetry unique in its identity and rarely excelled in its quality.

· 4 ·

Now and Then –
Father, Mother,
Friend, Self

THIS IS the story of a poetic life, but not of the life of the poet. Parts of the poetry may be biographical; parts certainly are not. The particular work at hand must come first, but sometimes there are new revelations as one follows differently colored threads through the fabric. One must read the individual poems —a long delight in itself—and then rearrangement reveals what was there all the time, a sort of spiritual or emotional autobiography somewhat like Wordsworth's *Prelude.*

In such a biography of the poet or the soul there are several levels of time—the moment of the original event, the meditations that follow soon thereafter, and the long-time recollections in agony or tranquility, sorrow or joy. What is not literally the story of a poet's life, then, may be very close to an autobiography of his inner life—his thoughts and reveries.

Besides Warren, no poet that I know of in the English language has written numerous poems that can be arranged to form a chronological account of much of the poet's life from youth to age. Tennyson perhaps did it, but always in a lyrical mode—never with clearly recognizable event and character. Some of Whitman's poems follow such a pattern in a loose fashion. Warren, however, has written poems that can be considered biographical not only about himself but also about his father, his mother, and his friend—or the poetic counterparts of these people. The biographical poems—much true and much imagined and designed—begin far back in talk and legend and proceed to the late moments of the poet's life in his most recent poems.

A number of complex structures simultaneously govern Warren's poetic accounts of his past. The interlockings of the poems are intricate. Within one poem there may be, for example, small parts designated with Arabic numbers; the small piece may be a section of a larger poem identified with a Roman numeral; the latter, in turn, may be part of a still larger work with a title to identify it. Warren writes some poems in "suites of three or four units." Even the titled long poem may be part of a book. Twenty-four separate poems are at once individual works and a unified book that Warren says in *Or Else—Poem/Poems 1968–1974* "can be considered a long poem, or it can be considered a group of short poems."[42] In the complexity of Warren's own organization of his poetry, it is possible to read the poems in many ways. All kinds of threads unify a single prespective in a diverse conglomerate.

The arrangement here is roughly chronological, beginning with the earliest events and proceeding to the poem about the latest event (or memory). All derives from Warren's personal or poetic past, springing from his childhood, proceeding to his poetic meditations at the time of the composition of the poem, and sometimes extending the subject of one poem into another piece written at a later date. One can follow the life of the father through three major poems, *Brother to Dragons* (the first extensive treatment in the poetry of any close member of Warren's family) to "Mortmain" to "Reading Late at Night, Thermometer Falling." Ruth Warren, the mother, died many years before her husband. With the passing of time, she became less a factor in the poet's day-to-day thoughts. But she appears in the poems, and she is often portrayed in her relationships with other people around her, or in less detailed characterizations than the father. The intensity of the emotions—given the distance of time—may be less, but not a great deal, and her early death seems to be the reason for the blurring.

The brother and sister of Warren appear in random glimpses and brief scenes or actions, never with characterizations in depth. Early in her young womanhood the sister, Mary, seems to have separated herself from the family, and she hovers as a remembered child over the poems but never as a living figure. Thomas was only nine years old when Warren went to Clarksville, and brothers separated by several years seem to develop close relationships only after a few decades have passed. Yet in many of the poems Thomas is there as a significant and silent figure, never speaking. Warren has said in his essay on Jefferson Davis and in personal letters that he and Thomas sit together, hunt together, and visit in silence—communicating deeply but without words.

Along with the Warrens and the members of the family of Grandfather Penn, one other person emerges intimately from the personal past—a silent friend, Kent Greenfield, star baseball player, hunter and fisherman, drunk, but a kindly child and a gentle man, who spoke with an old fashioned gentility. He first appears as the protagonist in a short story, "Goodwood Comes Back," but he is also in a marvelously inexplicable vignette when he kills a goose in *Brother to Dragons*. In *Now and Then* Warren writes a poem of broad reference, "American Portrait: Old Style"; the portrait is of Kent. A trip home usually meant a short visit to Kent, and a reminiscence of childhood and Guthrie in Warren's writings often contains an allusion to that boyhood playmate. In the essay on Jefferson Davis (1980) Robert and Thomas stand not only at the graves of their parents but also at the grave of Kent.

Moving through the narrative and meditations on intimates of Guthrie days is the character of Warren himself. He has written as many narrative poems as any major American poet. A Southerner, he is a born and bred and practicing teller of tales. But he is also one of the most explicitly meditative and lyrical poets in America, one of the most personal. He mixes his meditations on those close to him with overviews of the entire range of American history.

Though these autobiographical poems are not formally linked, no one of them can be fully appreciated in isolation. With sufficient annotation and explication, one might work out T. S. Eliot's "Mr. Eliot's Sunday Morning Service" for himself so that he might come to understand what happens as the persona sits in his pew and contemplates the actions of the priests and Sweeney in his bath. The poem does not require a knowledge of Eliot's religious beliefs and his biography. But that is not true of "Mortmain," because it involves Warren's actual father, the father in other poems, the father in the course of nearly a century of American history, the father as a meditator and even a would-be poet himself, and the diverse moods and meditations of Warren as son and as poet on the subject of his father.

A traditional poet may become intensely engaged in an attempt to penetrate the unfathomable past in a search for historical truth so far as it can be known. A descendant of an ancient New England family, Warren's friend Robert Lowell (an admirer of the Fugitives—especially of Allen Tate) has elaborately studied his heritage in such poems as "The Quaker Graveyard in Nantucket" and "For the Union Dead." But the relevance of Lowell's past for the poet's present is generally left mysterious, certainly not clearly stated by Lowell himself. Warren's fellow Fugitive, Tate, pursues the past, its meanings, and the search for self-assurance as strenuously and relentlessly as any modern poet. His poems go back to the origins of human awareness and consciousness ("The Wolves"), back to the classical past and the relevance of the ancients especially to the modern South ("The Mediterranean," "Aeneas at Washington"), and to the American past, which just might supply a meaning necessary for a poet who can define neither his world nor himself ("The Ancestors," "Mother and Son"). As a rule Tate and Ransom write about their acestors in their poems, but not about their parents.

Warren's poetry about his personal and family past, on the other hand, is extensive and detailed. He writes about himself, his parents, and his grandparents. Grandfather Penn talks about American history, especially the Civil War. The poet looks with his grandfather's and his own perspectives on the ancient American past. They arrive at decisions about the meaning of the world, and the absence of them.

The Frontier

Warren's poetic chronicle of the most ancient history begins with pioneers migrating, as the Warrens and Penns did, westward to Kentucky. "American Portrait: Old Style" has a protagonist called K (an obvious representation of Warren's childhood playmate Kent), whose character was out of harmony with the age; K should have been a frontiersman and an explorer. K and the boypoet wander at the first of the poem from the village to the woods, where they may find whatever reminders there are of the original settlers or travelers west.

The two boys find an "old skull" with an anonymous "stone-smack," apparently the cause of death. They go "past the marsh," where the skull was found, up the hill to a great oak tree, which had sheltered an early family moving to new homes in the West. Under the tree is what looks like a long-sunken grave, a six-foot depression. No artifacts of a settler's home, no cabin or well, remain under the tree. The boys conjecture that the "sunken grave" is evidence of a pause in the journey of pioneers: "So Pap must have died of camp fever, / And the others pushed on." This scene is the earliest encounter in Warren's poetry with the early history of the town of Guthrie and of the procession of American history. It anticipates the characterization of K as a should-have-been frontiersman.

The Late 1800s

History becomes deeply personal to the poet for the first time as he recreates the life of his father in the late nineteenth century. By poetic design certainly and perhaps partly by fortunate accident, his father appears in the poetry as a child in the earliest poem that develops a sustained portrait of a relative—*Brother to Dragons*.

In *Brother to Dragons* father and son take a journey to Smithland, the place of the violent events in the lives of Thomas

Jefferson's nephews in that poem. On the way to the plantation on the Ohio River the poet and his father (Robert Franklin Warren—Warren tells me that he was accompanied by his father on two or three trips to Smithland) pass by Cerulean, Kentucky, the birthplace and the home region of the father, and move "Through the landscape of his early experience. / We pass the land where once stood the house of his first light. / No remnant remains."

Setting out to observe Jefferson's nephews' plantations and to gain whatever perspectives they can, the poet and his father encounter the transience of human experience. The mystery is familial, personal, and historical. Father and son pass by that old Warren homeplace: "The house is a fiction of human / Possibility past." The ancestors are remote—even the father's father—"The grave of my father's father is lost in the woods." It does not take long for an unmarked grave to become lost, even when it is among other graves in a cemetery. But the grave in the poem is "lost," even though it once had a headstone. The lost grave fitted perfectly the context of *Brother to Dragons,* and when Warren wrote the poem he did not know where his grandfather was buried. Actually, the grave of the paternal grandfather is not lost, as Warren has since learned. W. H. Warren is buried in the cemetery in Cerulean, Kentucky, with a sizeable tombstone clearly marking his place of rest and his dates, 1839–1893. Even the grave of the great grandfather, named W. H. Warren also, is well marked in the same cemetery with clear dates, 1818–1864. Warren has never seen his grandfather's grave. Out of "ignorance," Warren says, and his father's mysterious silence about his family, he made the grave unmarked.[95] Nevertheless the grave seems to represent a significant but unidentifiable part of the scope of American history. The grave seems as remote as the other legends and the stories of *Brother to Dragons.*

The claim that the grandfather's grave is "lost in the woods" is a poetic and symbolic truth, far more important for *Brother to Dragons* than a genealogically informative tomb would be. One who knows familiar and ancestral facts is still compelled to guess the truth of the spirit. A grandfather who is actually buried in the known earth of a cemetery may be still metaphori-

cally "lost in the woods" of the mind and of history. Most of
the grandfather's childhood is lost to the memory of the father
and almost entirely lost to the son. "My father himself has, no
doubt, lost that orientation." Although the grandfather's grave
was not lost, "the event of hunting a grave in the woods actually occurred, before the Penn farm was sold," Warren has said.
"Father, who was a favorite of Grandpa, used to come there for
a week to pick up the family, and on one of these occasions,
when I was about 11 or 12 (I think they moved away around
1917), he took me on the grave-hunting expedition. I had the
impression then—or remembered it as such—that he was hunting his father's lost grave. But it must have been of some other
relative, maybe even great-grandfather. I can't remember. My
memory had played me a trick about it being a father's grave."[95]
After further thought, Warren concluded: "But there remains
the mystery of why he never showed me his own father's grave.
And told me nothing of him."

Actually, Warren has said, his father appears in *Brother to
Dragons* for the sake of the larger aims of the poem:

I want to see the poem in the modern world. I don't want to set it as
a historical poem, put it that way. I want a modern man, myself, you
see, and my father. I want such a relation too, myself, in time, with
my old father there, and older than he are these other people, back
there. I want a sense of a historical sweep, you see.[95]

At the end of the poem, after the rehearsal of all the mysteries
of the Jeffersons and the Lewises and of America as seen in the
Lewis and Clark expedition to the West after the Louisiana
Purchase had been made, the poet and his father again attempted to fathom the past. Here, as they looked at the land of
the father's birth, the father told the son how his own father
in each December had taken some "yellow percoon," a root,
mashed it, and put it in a jug of whiskey until it was given as
a medicine to the sons three months later at the beginning of
spring. It was a medicine, but it was also a ritualistic passing on
of some kind of gift or heritage from father to son—a plant and
a name known now only by a folk doctor.

When the son returns from his mountain-top trip to the home of the Lewises, again he recalls the percoon: "We have seen a small boy, wide-eyed, stand on the hearthstone / And accept, from his father's hand, the bitter dose of percoon. / The hearthstone [like the grandfather's grave] is gone whereon he once stood." The handing-on is the process of the changing of generations. The child, "wide-eyed," submissive, accepts the gift of the father. The acceptance is bitter, but it is also medicinal, with some kind of efficacy—now unknown. The father, Robert Franklin Warren, was never able to recall for his son what it was, and when I interviewed the son in 1979 he still had never learned what it was or is. The mysteries of the past are recollected by generations, but neither their identities, their purposes, nor their benevolent attributes may be known.

In a sense, Warren is writing about these characters based on prototypes in his family for two reasons—he is studying and creating a long historical view of the universal past; and he is reliving personally and intensely the most memorable and intimate moments of his life spent with his father and other members of his family.

Structurally, it is strange but effective for a poem, "Mortmain," to begin with the death of an American father in the twentieth century and to end with a vision of the same person as he had emerged momentarily from the woods during his childhood seventy-five years before. (The section is dated 1880.) The poet has a vision of his father's life, of the father-child who could not know his own future. *"Listen! . . . Listen! I know—oh, I know—let me tell you!"* But the boy-father remains in innocence. The knowledge is that of the son and the poet. "I know who he is, and would cry out. / Out of my knowledge, I would cry out." The images of the first two stanzas are extraordinarily well chosen to reveal the innocence of rural childhood. Everything points to birth in nature and suggests the movement of a child toward the responsibilities of the summer. There are pollen, "a powder of gold," dew in the "chartreuse coolness" of the inner flower of a tulip poplar. The boy shares the sacredness of beginnings and innocence: he is "hieratic, complete." He wears patched britches, a symbol of work and a simple if not poor rural life. One of the most famous boys of this kind in American poetry is Frost's swinger of birches, but Warren has a simpler environment even than the other youngster. He does not think of baseball, and the poem does not end (though both Frost and Warren can be explicit, too explicit and moralistic) with a meditation on the two worlds of mortality and immortality.

Early in the poem the boy emerges from the woods, but he is just on the verge of going into manhood. Instead of progressing toward some future goal with determination, he stands in "that idleness of boyhood / Which asks nothing and is its own fulfillment." His occupation is with a wand (suggesting childhood dreams and magic) of willow. At this point he can meditate, and there is no drive or demanding purpose in what he does. He and his task are "boy-idle and aimless."

The boy merely stands; the mature poet after the father's death looks back to the father the boy was and seems to urge him to leave his innocence and to confront the world and the process that end ultimately in the lifted hand of the deathbed gesture of "Mortmain." The boy remains "boy-idle and aimless" until the poet wishes to reveal to him whatever the long span of years of the lives of the father and son have told him. The poet first tells his boy-figure father where he is, "Trigg County . . . in Kentucky." The memory of the poet about his own past in later years in Trigg County is the subject matter of what he tells the recollected spirit of his father. The worlds of father and son differ a great deal. The father stood in the spring of the year, but the poet can "never remember the spring there." It is the drought of a summer or more mature years with "the pasture parched," and "the voice of the lost joree / [Is] Unrelenting as conscience, and sick, and the afternoon throbs."

Vainly the poet attempts to cross the parched pasture to the wonderful new woods of the child-figure of the father in the last stanza. The vision ends as the ancestral figure retreats to "The shadow of woods, but pauses, turns, grins once, / And is gone." The last line and a half of the poem are ambivalent; they belong clearly neither to the spring childhood of the father nor the summer adulthood of the poet: "One high oak leaf stirs

gray, and the air, / Stirring, freshens to the far favor of rain."
Warren calls these lines "a comment on the recollection" and
also "an image of tears (water) or a 'release.' "[95]

The girlhood days of the mother are made of gossamer images and thoughts, so other-worldly that they seem to have an
aura of the supernatural. "Tale of Time," Warren's longest
poem about his mother, is a mysterious recollection of bits and
pieces of her life and of people around her. The attitude of the
poem is much more questioning about her than Warren's poems
are about his father. Because of her much earlier death, time
seems more to have separated the mother and the son.

Part V in "Tale of Time" attempts to penetrate the past all
the way back to the mother's childhood—before the birth of the
poet, before her marriage, before the mother had groped her
way even through childhood to the relationships and puzzlements of young womanhood.

In each of the first three stanzas of Part V of "Tale of Time,"
the son asks her in an apostrophe long after her death what she
was thinking "at the whippoorwill hour," "when the evening
dove mourned," and when the "last saffron / Of sunset faded."
The setting, the place of her childhood, is identifiable by the
images. "Dark cedars" (also mentioned in each of the first three
stanzas) surround the house. Under them Gabriel Thomas Penn
sat when he talked to his grandson about the Civil War and
puzzled with him on why Dr. Knox did it. The child mother-to-
be in her wanderings has gone "beyond the dark cedars" to
think her long thoughts. She has stayed late until the "whippoorwill hour" when that almost-never-seen night bird begins
its solitary and penetrating calls in the darkness. "Lost in the
long grass," she has stayed until the darkness when the "sun . . .
sank." Whatever she thought about, she leaves her moment of
time and goes to the house where the lamps are "now lit." She
returns to the known, the domestic, the finite.

Like the first part, the second begins with three interrogative
lines (two questions in the second stanza, one in the first) and
ends with a similar leaving of the dark natural world and a
return to the domestic world where that ubiquitous old soldier
sire and grandsire sits "bent at his book." The first three lines

of the third stanza and the last of the fourth follow the pattern of questioning in a natural world and return to the human world. The son addresses his mother in her recollected or imagined childhood: "You found it necessary to go to the house."

The fourth stanza turns to statements: The girl "found it necessary to live on." She had a "joyous secret." But who, the poet might ask, can penetrate and identify the secret of a girl who long ago wandered between the house and "those sober recesses of cedar"? She lived into "our present maniacal century, / In which you gave me birth." Years later the poet, also a child, lay "in the grass of that same spot" and heard the inexplicable whippoorwill from "beyond the dark cedars." The images here point to sharings between mother and son; across many years and yet at the same ages of their lives they shared the same place—the home of the ancestral Penn, a place of beauty, search, and questions. If there are answers, they are not given, perhaps not remembered. The childhoods of the two parents exist in visions simple and wondrous of a past far beyond the realities and the ken of the poet.

"Mortmain" starts with an account of a rush to the bedside of a dying father and ends with the ambivalence of the vision, which suggests not only the ending of life at the beginning of the poem with a last-lifted hand and the ruck of sweaty bedclothes but also trials and struggles (as well as the love) between this time and the vision of the father's boyhood in Trigg County. "Mortmain" may be Warren's most accomplished family poem; certainly the lyrical presentation of the remote past of the father is in itself excellent—a personal and marvelous beginning of the chronicle of the Warren family.

In the father's beginning, in a way, come the ending of the poem and the ending of the poet's meditations on the long scope of the father's life. There is no hint about what will come next—doubling back again on the father's life or rushing ahead to the poet's own late years and his death. In the father's beginning is the end of the poet's meditations that came with the father's death.

As a single poem "Mortmain" begins with the death of the father and ends with the speculations of the poet about his father's emerging from the past, the frontier, and the psychologically puzzling mists of remote childhood. As a part of the poetic chronicle of Warren's ancestries, "Mortmain" covers as great a sweep as any poem he has written. The poem "A Vision: Circa 1880," Part V of "Mortmain," is beautiful in its own right, as part of a poem about the life and death of the father, and about its stage in the larger chronicle.

Part II, "A Dead Language: Circa 1885" is the first flashback after the moment of death in I. It is mostly accurate reporting of the struggles and hard labor of Robert Franklin Warren on the farm in the early years in Trigg County.

> Father dead, land lost, stepmother haggard with kids,
> Big Brother skedaddling off to Mexico
> To make his fortune, gold or cattle or cards,
> What could he do but what we see him doing?
> Cutting crossties for the first railroad in the region,
> Sixteen and strong as a man—was a man, by God!—

The spirit of the father as we learn of him from the memories of Warren and the life of that historical period is exactly right. Warren never knew the date of his grandfather's death or that the land was lost soon after his death, but Warren has never been one to stick to the actual fact when a detail will reveal an accurate truth of the heart or of history. Given the fact that Robert Franklin Warren began the hard labors of his late youth or first manhood just past his mid-teens, Warren has used "Circa 1885" as the crucial time. Robert Franklin Warren was sixteen. William H. Warren, his tombstone in Cerulean says, died in 1893—not "circa 1885." But child of a labor-worn father or orphan, Robert Franklin began his hard work in the days of the poverty-stricken, barely post-frontier days of the period just after the Reconstruction.

One thing only does he own, a Greek paradigm that foreshadows his yearning for knowledge and his love of literature and history. The simple paradigm is all he has retained of the Greek he always yearned to acquire from the books he bought and the tutors he hired. At sixteen he cut crossties with a double-bit ax, but by seventeen he began his apprenticeship in a lifelong career as businessman. He starts as a clerk in a "cross-roads store."

The first stanza of the account of the life of young Robert Franklin Warren glances first at his brother wandering on the frontier, "skedaddling off to Mexico." For each wanderer, there must be a worker—father or brother or son, an Odysseus and a Telemachus. As a young man, the poet's father was the worker who stayed at home. The attitude of his young life on the frontier becomes almost a brag in the manner of such divergent folk characters as John Bunyan or John Henry. "Cutting crossties," he "was a man, by God!" But the physical wonder is not enough because he works to the time of the Greek paradigm. And one year in the woods, wonders or no, is enough of that.

The father turns from the strenuous frontier to the black and dispiriting world of commerce. Following the material path of the Snopeses, but with an altogether different spirit, he carries his frontier dream into a country store—as Robert Franklin Warren was working in a store when he wrote the poems discovered years later by his son. The images are of prosaic needs, "piece goods and cheese, / . . . candy and plow-points." The season of the year is winter, and the mood of the young man who wishes to know and to learn is reflected in images of the dead time of the year. It rains, and the trees are black, and the water "in the ruts of the lane" is "sober as steel." Personally for the young man it is the time of ambition without opportunity. But whether he likes it or not, "That was that land, / And that was the life."

The third stanza begins with a second short passage of Greek —one of the passages quoted by the father to the son as he shaved.[95] He quotes the Greek and then translates and comments. "In the beginning / Was the word, but in the end was / What?" The word here is not the Messiah but the Greek of the father's unsatisfied longings. Looking ahead through the life of the man in all the poems, one knows that it is the word he will never attain. At this point the poem only asks: "In the end was / What?" A drastic shift of time occurs in the third stanza. Through the use of an image of a father (Robert Franklin now an older man) shaving before his son (Robert Penn) with a straight razor "big as a corn-knife" the poet recalls a memory that seems commonplace but is actually laden with meanings and suggestions: the manhood of a father and the childhood of a boy, the wonder of the child at the man, the closeness of parent and child. Shaving, the father recites the Greek for the beginning and the word for a second time in the stanza. Though the Greek springs from old frustration and disappointment, the father has triumphed in his failures. Family, joy in daily living, and fulfilling the obligations of routine labors enable the father to laugh "from the deep of a dark conquest and joy. / Said: 'Greek—but it wasn't for me. Let's get to breakfast, boy.' " The Greek and its glories are not forgotten, but regretfully relinquished in the father's joy in his son and in something seemingly so commonplace as breakfast. The poem conveys the intimacy of a son's memory of his father's love, and it also reveals the personal sacrifice exacted by the situation in the South in the decades before and after the turn of the century. But if the social condition was regional (whether or not Warren in the poem worked consciously from that perspective), the sacrifice is universal, as is the desire for knowledge symbolized by the fragment of Greek.

The explanation of the urge for Greek and all it symbolizes is partly stated by the father in "Reading Late at Night." As an old man, the father describes the compulsions of his youth: "When I was young I felt like I / Had to try to understand how things are, before I died."

About 1890, the dreams of the father in Warren's poems turned for several years to law, that pathway to power pursued arduously and sometimes futilely by many a young rural lad hoping for glory as a poet-lawyer. When the son was about twelve, say, in 1917, he discovered an old photograph:

> a young man
> In black coat, high collar, and string tie, black, one hand out
> To lie with authority on a big book (Coke or Blackstone?), eyes
> Lifted into space.
>
> And into the future.

It is a typical picture, whether of a young soldier posing with his rifle or his first gas mask, or of a graduate with cap and gown. But the future dreamed about in the photograph does not become the future in the fact. And old pictures renew the frustrations that assume added dimensions from the perspectives of later times. The boy is startled from his reverie of what his father had dreamed of being and what he might have been:

"Son, give me that!"

He took the photograph from my hand, said:

"Some kinds of foolishness a man is due to forget, son."

Tore it across. Tore
Time, and all that Time had been, across. Threw it
Into the fire.

The father's glimpse of the past leads first to anger and frustration. He throws the picture into the fire. Then he attains some kind of reconciliation: "I reckon that I was lucky enough to learn early that a man can be happy in his obligations." Years later Warren wrote that the incident and the comment are "not fiction."[95]

Then the poem shifts abruptly and immediately from the dream of law to the dream of poetry. "Later, I found the poems. Not good." Three times the father sought the promise of the word: in Greek, in the law, and in poetry. Three times he failed. The poet comments that "Man lives by images," but the father's images in dreams have failed. Each time he brought himself to some kind of reconciliation and acceptance while at the same time, through reading ("Reading Late at Night") he has kept up the struggle for the word, which is truth. As the poet says, "Truth is all." So Robert Franklin Warren, man and poetic character, struggled for all, and he never found it. But in each instance he preserved his integrity and recognized the worth of what he did find, though it was not "all."

Childhood—The Early 1900s

In the poetic glimpses of Warren's or the poet's personal and family past there are substantial gaps. Rather, one might say, the entire scope of the personal past is not so much a continuity as it is a series of mostly random vignettes, fragments of memory related in something of the fashion of clouds scuttling across the sky, separate but moving in the same direction and in similar colors and raggedy shapes. The largest gap in the chronicle occurs between the girlhood of the mother and the young manhood of the father on the one hand and the puberty and adolescence of the boy on the other.

One wonders about the cause of the gap: is it attributable to a human tendency not to know the details of the courtship and marriage of the parents and the infancy and early childhood of the narrator? I recall no novel of Faulkner that portrays fictionally the life of the novelist as a boy as it is portrayed in the printed memoirs of neighbors and friends and brothers. Sterne, on the other hand, shocked his readers in the eighteenth century by beginning his autobiography with an account of his conception and earliest days. Thomas Wolfe similarly starts *Look Homeward, Angel* with an account of the great events in the world at the time of his birth and continues from the perspective of a baby looking at a mammoth world from the floor. Is the gap—if there is one in most lives—psychological or literary or personal to Warren?

In the life of a writer, real and fictional or poetic, several reasons might account for a blank such as that between the 1890s and about 1914 in Warren's poems. Freud says that people recollect "the unimportant and accidental" and forget "the weighty and affective impressions" of the earliest years. Factors other than the psychological, it seems to me, are also at work in the lack of remembrance of things past. If anything is private and intimate, courtship is. The child—perhaps especially the oldest child like Robert Penn Warren—hears little family talk about the events that led to his parents' wedding, his begetting, the life of his parents before his birth (beyond the vital statistics and a few occasional and exceptional yarns), or their lives during his earliest years. Also, Warren comments, "The family had, I am sure, the old-fashioned habit of destroying letters—all kinds." But, Warren's mother, he says, "once told me two tiny incidents of her courtship and honeymoon—trivial and deeply moving."[95] Whatever the truth of these conjectures and regardless of the extent of his memories, Warren in his poetry has not written an account of the early years of his childhood.

In Warren's poetry, I find only one family event that might be autobiographical between the 1890s—ten years or more before the poet's birth—and 1917, when at twelve he found the picture of his father aspiring to be a lawyer. In "The Return: An Elegy" the poet goes home in his imagination to his mother's funeral. In grief and confusion, he sentimentally wished for one moment from his childhood: "turn backward turn backward O time in your flight/ and make me a child again just for tonight." The quotation from the popular poet Elizabeth Akers Allen is almost exact. The ironic recollection called up from the past and childhood is only one line long: "good lord he's wet the bed come bring a light." The desire for innocence turns into an unpleasant episode of embarrassment and physical discomfort. Of the poetry of childhood before the teens in Warren's poetry, that is all I find, and it is pure fiction. Warren says that he wrote the poem in the summer of 1935 "when I did not know that my mother was seriously ill."[95]

If the boyhood of Warren tended toward the bookish and the solitary, one relationship is a strong counter to all the reports of loneliness. The friendship with Kent Greenfield began when the Warren and Greenfield houses were in the country, just at the edge of town. In later years across decades there were fond and warm feelings between the two boyhood friends who became almost opposite kinds of men. Kent was a sort of big brother, about two years older than Warren, big and strong for his age. Warren was small for his age, and "Kent was the one who 'knew things'—woodslore, marksmanship, bird calls, etc."[95]

The poem about K (or Kent), "American Portrait: Old Style," is an "American" portrait, a poem about the adventures of founding a country. The old American past as it was known in Guthrie, Kentucky, had been gone long before. In the poem a teacher in the classroom refers to "The Dark and Bloody Ground," but all the boys can see of the old rich virgin earth and then the violence of the frontier is ruined country with "no

hope and no history here." So boyhood has to "invent it all"
—the adventure and the play about adventure. So they

> head out
> "To Rally in the Cane-Brake and Shoot the Buffalo"—
> As my grandfather's cracked old voice would sing it
> From days of his own grandfather.*

"American Portrait" begins as a poem about the campground of
westering pioneers, but the frontier has been reduced—even for
the boys—to shooting their mothers' chickens and to playing
frontiersman and Indian. But childhood's dreams are shorter
even than the days of the pioneer in the glorious lives of K and
the reminiscent poet.

> Yes, a day is merely forever
> In memory's shiningness,
> And a year but a gust or a gasp
> In the summer's heat of Time, and in that last summer
> I was almost ready to learn
> What imagination is—it is only
> The lie we must learn to live by, if ever
> We mean at all to live. Times change.
> Things change. And K up and gone, and the summer
> Gone, and I longed to know the world's name.

K or Kent the child only passes through the post-frontier
town. An American portrait now is not of a man on a Western
journey. He retains the spirit, the strength and grace, of the
older time: He "Seemed never to walk, but float / With a singular joy and silence." A man of action born later than his time,
he was "Polite in his smiling, but never much to say." "He
should have gone with Lewis & Clark, to the Pacific."[95]

---

*Warren writes in *Jefferson Davis,* page 2, that his grandfather sang "in his
old, cracked voice, one of the few songs that might rise from his silence, sung
only for himself, 'We'll Gather in the Canebrake and Hunt the Buffalo.'"

As the childhoods vanish, K goes on to his baseball and
booze, a cheap imitation of the big league pitcher he might have
become. The poet moves on toward "Time's jaw," where all the
teeth "snag backward." Youth passes, and the times and adulthood do not bring understanding to pitcher or poet. The end of
man in these instances is not, as the poet's father had said, "to
know." But the question is there even when the answer is not.
Father in other poems, and pitcher, and poet—all arrive at mysterious statements that describe the search but not the meaning.
Kent, the sensitive and thoughtful but unlettered man, the
ought-to-be frontiersman, asks a question exactly in the spirit
of the father—a question, Warren says, that came exactly from
Kent Greenfield himself: " 'But, Jesus,' he cried, 'what makes a
man do what he does— / Him living until he dies!' " He has not
found his answer, and all the splendors of childhood and its
play have not even made the question clear enough for the poet
to use a question mark instead of an exclamation point. The
place of the old frontier trench now has become "But a ditch
full of late-season weed-growth, / Beyond the rim of shade."
Even as an adult the poet lies "in the trench on my back,"
Warren says, "thinking of himself as dead," and sees the same
images without the longed-for explanations—"the late summer's thinned-out sky moves, / Drifting on, drifting on, like
forever." The poem of childhood in the country and of the two
boys ends mysteriously, as it must, with no answer, but with
a note of joy: "I love the world even in my anger, / And love
is a hard thing to outgrow." Here is perhaps at the same time
the most intimate and the fullest glance at the poet's joy in his
childhood play and sense of closeness with nature. It ends with
an encompassing look at history and at the world, but what the
poet yearns for is missing: knowledge and understanding.

Two poetic accounts of lonely events in the lives of Kent and
of Warren have been written. Both create moments of wonder,
almost Wordsworthian spots of time when it seems that one
may possess all glory in an instant of undefinable joy. Kent is
not a poet of talk and words, but of feeling and nature. His
moment comes from an unlikely place, like, say, "A ruined
mill / And millpond, wood lot, and a fox's den" in *Brother to*

Dragons. Something descends from the heavens, almost like a
meteor of fire on a burning bush:

> one wild goose that came one fall,
> Lost from its own that like a constellation
> Star-triumphing and steady thus bestrode
> The imperial cold altitude, and the hoots died south.
> Lost, sick, or old, it settled on a stock-pond,
> And heard the arrogant clamor darkling fade,
> And slept.
> Kent shot it just at dawn, threw down his gun,
> Crashed the skim-ice, and seized it, hugged it, ran
> Three miles to town and yelled for joy and every
> Step cried like a baby and did not know why.

Kent has experienced a moment of recognition, though he
cannot say what he has recognized. The bird is a thing of mystery, come from the unknown. Even the townsmen in the bar-
ber shop knew that: "From Canady, come all that way, well I
be durn." But Kent and the townsmen and the poet can only
marvel at the experience; they do not know what it means.
They have had feelings of transcendence and of possession, but
it is not given to them (and perhaps not to anyone) to know
what the possession is and what it means.

What happened with Kent and the goose recurs in greater
philosophical complexity in the story of the poet and a hawk
in "Red-Tail Hawk and Pyre of Youth," a poem written about
twenty-five years after *Brother to Dragons* and the account of
Kent and the goose. Again in a moment of solitude a youth
attains a pure moment of vision. Even if the denizens of the
opposite worlds are joined only for a moment, it is a time of joy
and perfection. In the first stanza the boy undertakes an ardu-
ous journey and climbs a "ridge crest" from which he can
survey the surrounding world. The horizon, "opening like joy,"
rewards the struggle of youth with the beauty and ruggedness
of nature. Ethereal and symbolic colors reveal the wonders of
the sky: "It was / The hour of stainless silver just before / The
gold begins." The boy has brought with him a rifle, which
hangs "on my hand / As on a crooked stick, in growing won-

der / At what it might really be." The gun has become more than a mere physical and manufactured object,and he seems not to "know its name." More than a rifle, it is a meaning, a nameless factor, even a spirit, an object that allows life to continue or doles out death. In these new and mysterious dimensions, the boy understands that "all is only / All, and part of all." In the sky world on top of the crest, beyond logic, "all is . . . part of all," or the finite all seen by the boy is part of some larger and infinite and therefore incomprehensible all. The boy sees

> A shadowy vortex of silver. Then,
> In widening circles—oh, nearer!
> And suddenly I knew the name, and saw,
> As though seeing, coming toward me
> Unforgiving, the hot blood of the air:
> Gold eyes, unforgiving, for they, like God, see all.

Many kinds of spiritual or religious terms in this passage describe the hawk: the vortex; the circles—like Platonic geometrical figures or emanations; the name—in folk motifs, as in the story of Adam in Genesis, to name is to possess; unforgiving—perhaps the vengeance of a divine being; the hot blood and the gold eyes—like a vision out of the Old Testament, maybe Ezekiel or Daniel. The boy is reminded that the eyes, "like God, see all"—again the *all,* but this time the infinite and the all-encompassing all. Truly now the bird is the prime and heavenly mover, "the center of / That convex perfection."

The American Indian novelist N. Scott Momaday says that eagles are omniscient, that they too see all; and the Jemez Pueblo Indians say that eagles bring the truths of heaven from God to man. The boy shares feelings like Kent's. Like Kent and perhaps also like the Ancient Mariner of Coleridge's poem (a subject of one of Warren's major critical triumphs), he attempts to possess by killing. It is a reflex. But it is also a wish to have and to know.

> There was no decision in the act,
> There was no choice in the act—the act impossible but
> Possible. I screamed, not knowing

From what emotion, as at that insane range
I pressed the cool, snubbed
Trigger. Saw
The circle
Break.

The poet rushes home as Kent had, living in a moment when
he wishes to tell all; but it is as impossible for the boy as it was
for Lazarus. "But nobody there." He looks at the glory he has
brought from the skies, and it is no longer there, "The lower
beak drooping, / As though from thirst, eyes filmed." The moment of loss and disillusionment is like the elements of those
folk stories of the kiss that makes a beautiful lover vanish or
of a wish ironically fulfilled in a way to bring not wonder but
horror. The glory is gone, and only taxidermy is left to attempt
to restore it. As in catching a dolphin or killing a bird, it is like
what an old fisherman musingly said, "Not all the arts of the
preserver or painter can hope to restore that color"—or the life
and the mystery.

The killer of the bird of heaven makes a valiant attempt, but
the human tools are humble.

My father's old razor laid out, the scissors,
Pliers and needles, waxed thread,
The burlap and salt, the arsenic and clay,
Steel rods, thin, and glass eyes. . . .

For a moment he dreams of success: "How my heart sang!" But
he fails because he has destroyed "the center of / That convex
perfection," and

In God's truth, the chunk of poor wingless red meat,
The model from which all molded, lay now
Forever earthbound, fit only
For dog tooth, not sky.

Thus the youth kills the hawk and the dream.

"Country Burying (1919)" is dated when Warren was fourteen years old. The stereotyped scene and the hot summer

setting convey the boredom of a boy forced to go to a funeral with his mother. According to the country custom in some locales, he was allowed to stay outside the church during services and merely to wait. So he sits "beyond the disarray / Of cars in the shade-patch, this way and that. / They stood patient as mules now in the heat of the day." The mother has expended the energy and endured the inconvenience to come to the funeral of a country woman unknown to her son and even "scarce known" to her.

" 'I respect her,' she'd said, but was that enough of a thing?" By implication, of course, it was. She is not a woman of town distinctions.

The two time levels in the poem—the past (the time of the action) and the present (the time of writing)—are distinct but inseparable in the poem. The funeral over, the poet and his mother leave, "the hole now filled." The poet moves away from the church and on to the world of maturity. From 1919 until the time of the composition of *Promises: Poems 1954–1956,* the situation and the time have continued unforgettable in the poet's mind. Years later "the heart gropes for center." Although he has known "voices and the foreign faces" and "dawn in strange rooms," he still realizes that one meaningful core of his life existed in his boyhood: his mother, the country people, and perhaps the country church he did not understand and perhaps will never comprehend, that world of "varnish, hymnals stacked, . . . painted paper on window glass." If he were to return, he reflects, he might enter, and he might attain more of the love and knowledge his mother had. But he is still uncertain: he *might* enter.

Even after all the years he might fail to understand and hear only a trivial noise: " *Why doesn't that fly stop buzzing—stop buzzing up there!"* The fly is first an indication of the mental state of the persona's searching. The end may be no more meaningful than the buzz. But the constancy of the sound also shows the relentlessness of the incomprehensible forces that cause the poet to attempt to fathom the present, the past, and whatever the buzzing fly may represent. Still he craves for the innermost meaning of existence, and the sound of the fly suggests both the search and the uncomfortable mental distraction. The poem is part of the biography of the mind, beginning in childhood and continuing in long-lasting unnameable speculations.*

The 1920s and the 1930s—The Mother

The youth of the father and his older philosophical puzzlings (perhaps a parallel to the life and thought of the poet himself) are the major paternal influences on Warren's poetry. About the mother he remembers most her associations with her neighbors and fellow citizens of Todd County. In "Tale of Time" a narrative about an insane pharmacist conveys also a sense of the mother's character from the eyes of the town and her son, the poet. Written about thirty-five years after her death, the poem begins by trying to recall her by remembering "the faces she saw every day." Despite long meditations, the forlorn poet is left (in a deliberately prosaic phrase, "in the lurch" because the faces "were part of her," and the loss of faces is a loss of "that much / Of her." The druggist is insane, but not too crazy to know that Todd County could do without some of the "folks that wouldn't be missed." Warren and Guthrie agree that "the druggist is not fiction. He did stop my mother to tell her she was safe. Then he was sent to a state asylum."[95]

"Tale of Time" begins with Part I, "What Happened"—the death of the mother and the subsequent thoughts and the rituals. Times, as people say, are bad. It is October, fall, the season of death. Ruth Penn Warren died in October, 1931. Also, "It was the Depression." The season is also a time of harvest, or of the failure of the harvest, or of good crops but no market. The people suffer, death or no death, and no authority can prevent the suffering even with good intentions: "Hoover was not a bad / Man." The first stanza ignores the actual death of the mother except in three blunt words. "My mother / Died." If Hoover cannot avoid troubles, even God may not prevail:

*"This poem," Warren says, "goes with 'Amazing Grace.' " There are a number of similarities, but a number of contrasts as well.

"God / Kept on, and keeps on, / Trying to tie things together, but / It doesn't always work."

Stanza two also states the death once and bluntly: "We put the body / Into the ground." Then the distractions quickly come again. Indeed, the burial may cause them. Images of finality and death in nature distract the poet from thoughts of his mother's death and at the same time remind him of it—darkness (the end of day) and "the last oak leaf of autumn" (oak leaves are among the last to die in the fall). The gold of the leaf and the gold of sunset join in great pain (even in beauty) *"beyond* the pain one can ordinarily / Get" [italics mine].

Evening comes after the filling of the grave (in Warren's blunt language, "the clod's *chunk*"), and the poet attains realization before midnight when he goes "to the bathroom for a drink of water." In the intensity and monotony of grief he stares at his face; probably with surprise, he sees no tears; he thinks of copulation (perhaps creation, maybe his own in the womb of his mother; perhaps his own casual fornication); he meditates on water "deeper than daylight"—beyond the penetration of light and thought—and of woods just as deep (remember the woods of the mother's early child hood—see Part V, "What Were You Thinking, Dear Mother?"); he associates life and death in his meditations ("Blood on green fern frond"); he recalls Christian terms, "the shedding of blood" and he doubts all—even the meaning of his "own experience." From the momentousness of religion, he turns again to the inappropriateness of sex at this moment of grief and tries to "think of a new position." In frustration and confusion, he makes no connection between sex and creation. He puzzles over whether his thoughts are grief and decides that his ramblings are "no doubt the typical syndrome."

The poem ends with the prophecy that "There will also be the dream of the eating of human flesh." The poem has progressed from a look in the mirror to what seems to be cannibalism. But it is not that. Instead, it is a sort of mortal, earthly, and human Eucharist or communion. Literally, the metaphor suggests, over a long period of time the poet will absorb into himself his mother and her memories. That union which results from the spirit of the dead becoming a part of the spirit of the living is what is meant by "the eating of human flesh." The first part of "Tale of Time" begins with the separation of the dead mother and the mourning son; it ends with the mother becoming more than ever before a part of the living son.

"What Happened" in "Tale of Time" is really the second account of the poet's return to the death and burial of his mother. The first, "The Return: An Elegy," was a part of Warren's first volume of poetry. "The Return," Warren has written "was pure fiction"; it was begun when Warren received a letter from his father reporting that his mother was "not feeling well" but "expressing no grave concern." Then she grew progressively worse as Warren traveled to Guthrie, and she died a day or two after Warren arrived home. He watched her "slowly sliding toward death," but he did not know until near the end what is at least suggested in the poem—that his mother was dead or dying.

The two poems about the death and burial of the same person (one based on fiction, one on reality) could almost have been written by two different poets, even though Warren believes that the late poem was "somehow indebted to 'The Return' in a number of ways." The older poem is more general, less explicit about the image resulting from the experience, less respectful, more shocking, more full of details not obviously related to the death, perhaps more self-centered. The second is more personal, more openly dramatic and introspective, fuller of grief, more aware of religious and philosophical implications. Some of the superiority of the later poem, I believe, may be due to the fact that it was, as Warren says, "not fiction."[95] These two poems on the same subject by a young poet and the same man years later suggest in many ways the maturing processes of both a man who loved and who wrote poetry.

The center of "Tale of Time," Part IV of six parts, is a reverie entitled "The Interim." It is the moment between "the clod"—the burial—and "the private realization," a moment of contemplation. This middle of the poem is an account of the family without the mother. Vicariously, the deceased mother is represented by her former helper, a servant, an old black woman who

had worked in the home. After the funeral the family in "Tale
of Time" walks over the railroad tracks to the home of the sick
and dying old woman who had spent much time with the
mother. In the manner of Eliot's *Four Quartets,* Warren writes:
"Between the beginning and the end, we must learn / The nature of being, in order / In the end to be." Surely, they seem
to think, if anyone knows "the nature of being," it will be the
old dying woman. "The episode about the visit to the old dying
woman," Warren says, "is as straight reporting as I could make
it. It just fell out that strange—and to me—wonderful way."[95]

> She
> Whom we now sought was old. Was
> Sick. Was dying. Was
> Black.

Certainly her status reduces matters to their barest essentials.
"This episode," Warren has written, "is *not* fiction, even in
detail. Seeley (Cecilia) had been a nurse and then until she got
married, our cook. The relationship was very close with the
family. Father had always done things for her."[95]

The family in the poem—a father, a brother, and a sister
(identical in make-up to the Warrens)—yearn to know. The
poet asks "Is / Existence the adequate and only target / For the
total reverence of the heart?" That is to say (if the poet has not
been explicit enough himself), Is living the only thing worthy
of admiration, indeed worship? The black woman ought to
know. She has known the mother and held the poet in her arms.

He asks "what love is," and after a detailed description of the
Negro district, Squiggtown, he accuses: "You have not answered my question." The poet seeks his answer from a strange
source: a dying woman propped up because she cannot breathe
lying down. The desired oracle is a "black / Aperture in the
blackness which / Was her face." The eyes, holes that "bubble
like hot mud," cannot see the asker of the question. As the hand
of the father rises in an inexplicable gesture of meaning in
"Mortmain" as he dies, so the hand of the black woman "rises
in the air. / It rises like revelation." It reveals nothing, however,

or only a little. "The voice says: *you.* / I am myself. / The hand has brought me the gift of myself." But not the gift of an answer. In a moment of intense emotion at this second encounter with death in one household in one day, the young man kisses the black cheek, and the father leaves a twenty-dollar bill and also kisses the cheek.

The father after they leave asks one of the stark questions —or perhaps all of them are the same question—he and Kent have often asked in the poems: *"Oh, God, what / Is twenty dollars when / The world is the world it is!"* The sister weeps, but in this long visit to the dying black woman the poet so far has only collected the "factors to be considered in making any final estimate."

Part 6 only promises a solution and provides images that are the context of the indefinable "fugitive thought." Part 7 meditates with no result on "Time" and "History" and looks toward more reconsiderations. The "solution" is given in Part 8, and it adds something to the mystery of Section I of "Tale of Time," to "the dream of the eating of human flesh." So:

> You
> Must eat the dead.
> You must eat them completely, bone, blood, flesh, gristle, even
> Such hair as can be forced.

That is the ultimate communion, religious or secular, human and divine, or human and human.

Surely even the first communion must have been in some ways repulsive. The disciples were told to eat Christ's flesh and to drink his blood. The longest section of "Tale of Time" also stresses revulsion. And death. The union is with a dying old black. If there is communion or union at all, it must be overcome in a ritual uniting all. The love of the servant in the days of the youth of the poet culminates in this terrible complete eating of the worst parts—"flesh, gristle, even . . . hair." Given that final act, Part 8 of Section IV, "The Interim," prepares for conclusion and knowledge, even hope. "Immortality is not impossible. / Even joy." Once hope and joy are attained, the poet can return to the beautiful memories of his mother and her childhood, Section V, "What Were You Thinking, Dear Mother?"

Through the meditations of these first five sections, the poet ultimately arrives at the last poem of "Tale of Time"—VI, "Insomnia." He contemplates a ghostly return to that "Place of grass" and to the "hour of whippoorwill." To the place of his mother's childhood (something like the old Penn place in Cerulean) and the time of his mother's childhood where he saw her in Section V in a vision after her death—"at the whippoorwill hour, lost in the long grass" and in the "darkness of cedars." He thinks of returning now, not a child, of a reunion over distances and time. The mother left when the son-man was not looking: "a man cannot keep his eyes steadily open / Sixty years."

In the insomnia of the night after the death and the long latter part of the poem, the poet continues his speculations about the unknowable in the afterlife of his mother. The soul and the corpse mingle in a vision:

> Oh,
> What age has the soul, what
> Face does it wear, or would
> I meet that face that last I saw on the pillow, pale?

If Warren is an unbeliever and a yearner, he spends a great number of lines on the questions forever in the minds of believers and doubters.

> The dead,
> Do they know all, or nothing, and
> If nothing, does
> Curiosity survive the long unravelment?

I take "unravelment" to be the slow process of dying and decay —"long" because it may continue through all the later years of life. Warren writes: "This echoes questions raised early by the Church Fathers."[95] Curiosity also refers to the wish—perhaps even demand—for definition after death. If it is an emotion of the soul after death, it is curiosity about life before death, and the nothing they know is perhaps a forgetfulness of the soul about the events of life before death. The dead, then, in whatever eternity there is, may not remember their own past or the living.

The poet wishes to know about the dead (working his way through his grief), and he asks "what they think about love." The speculation leads to no answers. Life before death of a loved one is more finite and determinable than the post-death world of ethereal shadows. The poet can know more about it. The minds (or hearts) of the living are mortal and therefore self-centered. Grief cannot remove the self from the grieving, and "I / Know now at long last that the living remember the dead only / Because we cannot bear the thought that they / Might forget us." The demand that the dead remember back through the beyond to the person of the son and the poet is mortal and egocentric. It is a demand for continued identity in the past and in the mind of the dead mother. But the grieving and uncertain poet doubts: "Or is / That true?" He has a sudden wish to tell his undefinable soul of his mother "all that has happened to me." But he does not himself know what has happened.

In a poem that avoids triteness only by ambiguity, he sleeplessly meditates on

> all the interesting things
> That must have happened to you and that
> I am just dying to hear about—
>
> But would you confide in a balding stranger
> The intimate secret of death?

No, she cannot. Now the mother and son belong to different worlds and generations. Besides the impenetrable barrier between the living and the dead, the living cannot know that ultimate and "intricate secret" without themselves undergoing the process of dying.

This insomniac griever in the last section of "Tale of Time" continues this line of unanswerable questioning: "Does the soul have many faces . . .?" If the poet entered the world of death, would he see the child's face, or that of the young mother, or of "Glimmer in cedar gloom . . .?" Again Warren had in mind the Church Fathers, he says. The poet, now older than the mother-child "will ever be" offers to take her from the long grass and the dark woods—of the past, of childhood, of death. He will take her "back home, they're waiting." The poet stops at the edge of the woods (perhaps the border between life and death) and watches her until she enters the house (perhaps a house with multiple meanings—"including no doubt," Warren says, "the farmhouse in which the father [Old Penn] could be reading by his lamp)."

When she enters, grief—the emotion of this mortal and insomniac night of her burial—returns and the son hears "night crash down a million stairs." He finds it difficult to breathe. Grief, a hand, will "compress / The heart till, after pain, joy from it / Spurt like a grape." The death has brought some glimmer of truth, and this time the poet himself arrives at one of those statements uttered in other poems by Kent or the poet's father: "Truth / Is all." It has come from the death of the mother, and it must be spoken "Slowly, in a whisper . . . never spoken aloud." Whatever it is, it is not spoken in the poem by the spirit of the mother or the grieving son. After all, hard as it is to accept, the emotions and reactions can only be felt—they can never be said. They cannot even mean until death. Unlike poems that can *be*, these meanings may not even *be* until they are known at the edge of the woods or in death.

In the sequence of the poetic biography or autobiography, the insomnia and the meditations on the death of the mother are followed by another stanza (in "Red-Tail Hawk and Pyre of Youth"), this one more despairing than the grief in "Tale of Time." During the last night of his life in his childhood home and bed ("there for the last / Time I lay"), the young man lies with "whiskey / Hot in my throat." He thinks of the hawk and, by implication, of his mother. Somewhere, he knows, the "yellow eyes" are staring "in vengeance." In the insomnia of "Tale of Time" he had learned that God could forgive. The hawk, or his shooting of the bird, has provoked more questions. *"Was* it vengeance" in the stare of the hawk? "What could I know?" Since the night of the burial of his mother, he has begun to contemplate both the natural and the supernatural. "Could Nature forgive, like God?" The poet's failure to continue the questioning and to arrive at answers or even speculations about the answers reveals less certainty and more skepticism than he felt after the death of his mother.

Memories of his mother came to Warren in brief flashes and in passages or short poems even in his older years. One poem from *Being Here* (1980) is a memory of his mother not long before she died. The Allen Tates brought their baby Nancy and "stashed" it "with Grandma while they went East for careers."

> So my mother seized it,
>
> And I knew, all at once, that she would have waited all day,
> Sitting there on the floor, with her feet drawn up like a girl,
> Till half-laughing, half-crying, arms stretched, she could swing
>   up her prey
> That shrieked with joy at the giddy swoop and swirl.

But the moment in the poem is brief. Then mother and son walk the streets of the town. "She laid out my supper. My train left at eight / To go back to the world where all is always the same." After all the years in this last volume, there is no notable event to remember, only the passing of the time long ago and the mood.

The 1940s and the 1950s—The Father

The lives of the mother, the father, the friend, and the poet all follow the natural progression from the joys of discovery, to unfulfillment and failure, to the last regrets and death. The death of the mother begins the endings in the early thirties; the puzzlements that follow derive briefly from the unblinking yellow eyes of the hawk. Then come many accounts of the long life and decline of the father, always a man of reading and speculations. He had to follow a commercial career. The bank in which Robert Franklin Warren was an officer failed before his wife's death; he "struggled a few years after her death, then was forced—he always felt it unnecessary—into bankruptcy."[7] "Reading Late at Night, Thermometer Falling" begins with the physical and intellectual decline of the father. The season and the night, like the life, are cold. The heat has been turned off: "The radiator's last hiss and steam-clang done," and the light comes from the discomfort of a "bare hundred-watt bulb that glares / Like truth." But still in the night and late in his life he props his book on his blanket and reads. All nature is frozen: Even "the tendons / Of a massive oak bough snap with the sound of a / Pistol-shot." This aging scene is the culmination of that wish of the youth who "Had to try to understand how things are, before I died." The father reads as he has all his life: Hume, Roosevelt, a Greek reader, Freud, a psychology text-book, history, college textbooks, and even a book on law.[95] But in his old age he still does not "understand how things are."

The son's dreams inspired by the hawk and the father's aspirations that arise from the books are similar in some ways. The dead hawk ("feathers shabby, one / Wing bandy-banged, one foot gone sadly / Askew, one eye long gone") stands watch over the lumber room long after the poet has left home. The hawk presides over the aging process of the poet and the end of his youth. So the son lights a match and makes a pyre of the hawk and other items of younger days—suggesting, perhaps, a part of the process of his reaching the conclusion that he, like his father, will not "understand how things are." The poet has been gone from his childhood home for years, and this is a "ritual cremation" for the hawk and all it represents. The burn-ing of the hawk, Warren says, came during "the bankruptcy period" and occurred during "the last night [he spent] under that roof."[95]

The image of the burning hawk brings the poet to a full realization of the end of his youth. The "shape designed godly for air," the hawk that has stood in the study for years, falls, and the poet can do nothing but think and "walk in the dark, and no stars." He foresees now his own death and even prays that in that last trip down the hospital hall he will see the glory he felt in the moment of the killing of the hawk: "the first small silvery swirl / Spin outward and downward from sky-height / To bring me the truth in blood-marriage of earth and air." The implications of that marriage in a moment of death and life are all: "earth and air," as the poet says; here and hereafter, perhaps; mortality and immortality; "unjoyful joyousness"; and all the other paradoxes and contradictions. Ultimately, it is not possible to know. The moment of death for the poet blends in the moment of death for the hawk. In a "dazzling moment" the intense ecstasies of life will mingle: the ecstasy of the youth's feelings at the time of the killing of the bird, the fire of the burning of the poor stuffed bird, and perhaps, the indescribable agonies and blisses that come to pass in the transformations of the ultimate end.

One of the most peaceful passages in all of Warren's writing occurs when the poet remembers in *Brother to Dragons* a time of intimacy between the father and a grandchild (probably Warren's niece, Tommie Lou, before he had any children of his own). It is "Sunday afternoon, / . . . after the chicken dinner and ice cream"—apparently always a moment of tranquility in a Warren household since Robert Penn's childhood days. The grandfather is engaged in his old preoccupation—language, the rudiments of Greek and Latin, the symbols of knowledge.

> I saw him sit and with grave patience teach
> Some small last Latin to a little child,
> My brother's child, aged five, and she would say
> The crazy words, and laugh, they were so crazy.
> There's worse, I guess, than in the end to offer
> Your last bright keepsake, some fragment of the vase
> That held your hopes, to offer it to a child.
> And the child took the crazy toy, and laughed.
> I wish you would tell me why I find this scene so sweet.

The poet has found an image that combines innocence and the eternal search for knowledge. In the last line, however, he seems to renege; unable to interpret the scene himself, he calls on the reader or the impersonal "you" to interpret for him. When the

poet revised *Brother to Dragons* twenty-six years later, he made
no change; he had not yet arrived at the words for the sweetness
of the scene. Some ecstasies are beyond articulation. But he did
find a way of increasing the intensity: he added a break and
made the one line that expresses his wish a one-line stanza,
separate unto itself.

The closeness of the family, the similarity of the search for
knowledge in the son and the father, is shown by the son's
taking his father with him to the scene of the crime of the
nephews of Thomas Jefferson. The age and lack of physical
strength of the father—and perhaps the reconciliation he had
long before learned to accept—left him drowsing in the car "For
he had climbed his mountains long ago, / And met what face
—ah, who can tell?" The son, "a God-damned fool," he calls
himself, searches for truth at the Lewis home in the awful heat
of a summer's sun on top of the Lewises' bluff. But he does not
find the explanation of the sweetness of grandfather and grand-
daughter—of the love across the gap of generations—instead,
he discovers the black snake, the dragon, "the ictus of horror"
in us all. "The real snake, a bastard," Warren says, "reared up
(you can't invent this! Love God and he'll send it)."

The last glimpses of the father before his death in the poetry
are still of the search—the reading, and his accompanying the
son on his own search for the truth of the violent crime of
Jefferson's nephews. In the scene of the old father in *Brother to
Dragons* (ironically the first explicit appearance of the father in
the poetry and also the last extended association between father
and son before the death) the search for truth by the father had
become merely the idle curiosity of the bystander as the son
carried out the active search.

Then the father's death.

The first news of the death in the poetry comes in a title for
the first section of "Mortmain"—written in the cryptic style of
a telegram or of a secondary headline composed by a wordy
journalist: "After Night Flight Son Reaches Bedside of Already
Unconscious Father, Whose Right Hand Lifts in a Spasmodic
Gesture, As Though Trying to Make Contact: 1955." (Robert
Franklin Warren did die in 1955.) The poet's account of his

father's death is true.[95] The strange style of the title of this elegiac poem suggests the impersonality and the ordinariness of the way death messages bring their unabsorbable news. The sudden message, the hasty arrangements for the flight, the meandering thoughts of the son on the way to the scene gather themselves together in an inexplicable gesture: it is spasmodic, sudden, brief, perhaps involuntary. Who is to know? The father seems to try to "make contact," and the son can never know what was mental effort and what was merely muscular.

Death is not comfortable. The father lies on a "sweated sheet" in a "ruck of bedclothes ritualistically / Reordered by the paid hand / Of mercy." Perhaps there is greeting in the hand, but the son sees the past. "Like law, / The hand rose cold from History / To claw at a star in the black sky." Ambivalence prevails in every image: the law yearned for by the young man decades before and the natural law of biological movements; the hand that rises from the history studied by the father all his life or from the past of mankind and, more personally also, of father and son; the clawing of the terrible struggle in frontier times and for knowledge and also the clawing for whatever the dying man may struggle for at the moment of death; the star of aspiration and of the unattainable; the black sky of the nature of the world and of the darkness of death just ahead. The image, Warren says, is "also an echo of childhood when the 'father is law.'"[95] The son watches how the "white hand ... / Lifts in last tension of tendon, but cannot / Make contact."

Suddenly there is contact—at least in the mind of the poet. The sad ironies like those in the terrible nursery rhymes in the first edition of *You, Emperors, and Others* return and link the memories of the poet and the churnings of the dying heart of the father: *"oh, oop-si-daisy, ... / oh, atta-boy, daddio's got / One more shot in the locker, peas-porridge hot—"* The heart-rending sight of the dying father mingles with memories of the joy and the vigorous movement of the times of active play and the singing words of the accompanying nursery rhymes.

Then the "hand sank," and all fell with it—"The failed exam, the admired endeavor, / Prizes and prinkings...." And innocence. "Back of the Capitol, boyhood's first whore—" The red-light district in Nashville was called "back of the capitol."[95]

At the moment of the father's death, remembering his love and his search, the son stands "Naked in that black blast of his love." So endeth the life of the father, but in one more part of "Mortmain" and in three parts of "Reading Late at Night" the memories of the father live on with the son.

The main memorabilia of the father other than his human descendants are the old Greek books, those symbols of the knowledge he sought always. They stand for the man and his hopes, in the main thwarted over and over by all the years, but never beyond reconciliation and never to the point of defeat in his life. Time after time they recur in the poems. When Warren and I talked before a fire at his home in January, 1979, he told me he wished to show me the old books and one of them he had just recently found. These truths of the hearts of the father and son may show very little analytically about the art of the poems, but they reveal a great deal about the desires, feelings, and sincerity of both men—and those, after all, are basic components of the lyricism of poetry.

As an image of his father's yearnings, Warren uses fox-fire, that luminescent glow of decaying wood deep in a forest, as strange as the passing years. He dates "Fox-Fire" in 1956—one year after his father's death, but he begins the poem "Years later." One year from the death, but a lifetime of years after the beginning of the dreams of the father. In reminiscence, he sees his father through images and symbols of age—a yellowed Greek grammar, the face of night, ashes flaking from the firelog, and a sky bleeding a dull red in one small spot. "I hold the book in my hand, but God / —In what mercy, if mercy?—will not let me weep. But I / Do not want to weep. I want to understand." His father wanted to know; the son wants to understand. There is little difference except the perspective of time. Just to "state the problem" would move toward solution. "If once, clear and distinct, I could state it, then God / Could no longer fall back on His old alibi of ignorance. / I hear now my small son laugh from a farther room." The implications of the sudden switch in generations are many, though none of them are more than implications. With the grandson and son the processes of life and death are beginning again. There will be new yearnings. But there is laughter, perhaps of infancy and perhaps, also, of the hopes of a time that may transcend some of the hardships of the frontier life of the grandsire.

The poet puts aside the old book—beside his own Greek grammar—and leaves, knowing

> that all night, while the constellations grind,
> Beings with folded wings brood above that shelf,
> Awe-struck and imbecile, and in the dark,
> Amid History's vice and vacuity, that poor book burns
> Like fox-fire in the black swamp of the world's error.

Whatever the folded wings are—supernatural spirits, the son's grievings over the strivings of the father, the emotional awareness of the similar links between generations—"that poor book burns / Like fox-fire" with its own self-generated light. The yearnings of the dead ancestor do not yield without light to the "black swamp of the world's error."

Parts 5, 6, and 7 of "Reading Late at Night"—also a sort of elegy—are apostrophes to the dead father. A man, Warren says, cannot address a dead father "on a matter / As important as this when you were not dead." Now, nearing the end of the grief of many days and poems, he addresses his father "for the last time." Not sure of what he can say, he calls his talk "Indecipherable passion and compulsion"—"indecipherable," yes, but a cipher has meaning whether or not one breaks the code. It is not "habit, tic of the mind, or / The picking of a scab." It is not involuntary; it is summoned—not a jerk of the knee at the blow of a rubber hammer.

The son, glancing at his own successes and failures, recalling what he made of his own old yellowed grammar, remembers the life declaration of his old father, a long one-liner in the poem: "I've failed in a lot of things, but I don't think anybody can say that I didn't have guts." Comparing himself to the father, the son forgives his father of all, "Even your valor." The valor was great. For eighty-six years the father, except for one illness, never "spent a day in bed." In truth, Warren says, Robert Franklin Warren "had one illness when I was about 6."[95] But he cried out at last—and "they discovered your precious secret: / A prostate big as a horse-apple."

So "The past . . . / Glows forever." But the son cannot grieve forever. Time remains, and another time changes. "Tonight snow is predicted. This, / However, is another country." The post has taken a line from Marlowe (also used by Eliot and Hemingway). "That was in another country," they wrote, "and besides, the wench is dead." It is at long last in this poetic life the father who is dead.

The 1970s—The Friend

Given time and the usual course of events and mortality, without accidents, the son and the friend survive the father. The last specifically (though partially) autobiographical poem of the sequence returns to K—playmate, now old, of Guthrie—great man and a weak one. Strong, frail, but beloved.

K never made his journey west,[109] but he did leave the birddogs he loved. Instead of going to the frontier, he went to "The Big Leagues, . . . a fool game." The girls "popped gum while they screwed," and the spectators, children in fact or at heart and ignorant of K's world, "hadn't yet dreamed what / A man is, or barked a squirrel, or raised / A single dog from a pup." Like the father and the son, K yearned, but for the knowledge of the woods instead of the books. Warren has said:

Before Kent had drunk himself out of pitching for the Giants, he at first leased a rundown farm in Connecticut, brought his bird dogs up, and bought 500 (or maybe more) ringneck pheasants, and spent every free moment out there. Then McGraw caught on and made him give up the farm and send those "God-damned dogs back where they belong." K said he always got up with the sun, and in New York there was nothing to do till the game. "Liked girls plenty," but "a girl can't take up your whole time." So he was lost, until he found a gymnasium that opened at 8:30 A.M. Then swam a mile, did bar bells, ran a mile, played pick-up basket ball—till McGraw caught on, and chewed him out, saying he wouldn't be fresh for the game. "If I ever catch you in

a gym again, you are fired. Put your mind on pitching." "Well," said
K to me, "you just can't ride hotel lobbies. Not all morning, and I never
read a book I didn't have to, and I hate movies, not real enough for
me." So he took to morning-drinking. "Now night drinking never hurt
anybody. But morning drinking and you really aren't fresh for the
game." So season by season he couldn't last, and that finished him.
Came back and really went into the gutter. Black whores in Squigg, etc.
Then World War II and the draft took him off likker.

The long years pass, and the necessary separation of friends
is a part of the years. The poet returns to the town and goes to
see the friend. His home is a place of love, especially of un-
speakable understanding between animal and man. K is at
home "With the bird dogs crouched round in the grass/ And
their eyes on his eyes as he whispered / Whatever to bird dogs
it was." (I saw them too, once, in 1977, less than a year before
Kent died. Their tongues out, they looked anxiously backward
at me as they trotted toward the fields in their hope for a hunt.)
    The greetings of the poet and the older American are casual,
concealments of memories and feelings that neither knows how
to say. On this visit of Warren to Guthrie, Kent relived a moment of his old glory. After Kent returned to Guthrie, he and
Warren

were passing some old men on a hot afternoon, sitting before a black-
smith shop. We overheard one old bastard say, "There goes the Greenfield boy. Done drunk his chances up. Throwed 'em away." K. turned
around, and called out "Look here," and suddenly was cold sober,
swung down for a stone and pointed to a pole some way off. Said:
"Look," wound up and let fly. Right on target. Turned around and
called: "Still got control, Boys." So we went on.[95]

Even with just a rock and after his failure, Kent's triumph was
like Babe Ruth's promise of a homer with a pointed finger over
the stands. Kent told me that he destroyed the insulator *before*
he left Guthrie and played baseball in the major leagues. It was
a sign of vigor and the exuberance of youth. In "American
Portrait" Warren has changed the time of the episode by many
years, however, and placed it *after* the brief success and the

years of frustration—at baseball and a world with no real place for K. Poetically, it is a sign of defiance and of triumph in the old skill after a half century of meditating on "what makes a man do what he does." At least he still has control—some, anyway. In pride, in defiance of his failure, he proved again the old talents.

> Like young David at brookside, he swooped down,
> Snatched a stone, wound up, and let fly,
> And high on a pole over yonder the big brown insulator
> Simply exploded. "See—I still got control!" he said.

In "American Portrait: Old Style" the poet wanders back years later to the old sunken grave—the worn trench of childhood and the frontier, now "But a ditch full of late season weed-growth." Nobody is there—no frontiersmen, no children playing, no men. The poet lies on his back in the grave and sees the sky move, "Drifting on, drifting on, like forever." He puzzles on "What it would be like to die"—as mother and father have died, and as K and he and all will. There is the faint suggestion of fox-fire in the swamp from the decaying old skull of the early frontiersman killed on the journey west.

Warren ends this poem about his childhood with an affirmation: "I love the world even in my anger. / And love is a hard thing to outgrow." It is a love despite his failure—as his father had failed—at the aim of man to know. And love though he has, he has not answered K's question, "What makes a man do what he does— / Him living until he dies." There may not be answers, but at least there is love and a question.

The 1970s and the Past

Part V of "Tale of Time" consists of a similar vision—but of a much older time—of the poet's mother, emerging from the woods and preparing to enter a world different from her childhood. A contrasting vision is the subject of one of the poems of *Or Else*. Published in a volume in 1974, it is a poem about all the members of his family; mostly it is a picture of death, a still time that has passed. Warren calls it "I Am Dreaming of a White Christmas: The Natural History of a Vision," but it is not any particular Christmas that ever happened, and whatever history may be found in the poem is only ironically "natural." The time never happened except in the mind of the poet, who is a dreamer about worlds forever lost to him.

This dream world is not a place to be entered without great pause and considerations. The poem, in fact, begins with a threat and a fear—in italics. *"No, not that door—never!"* But the poet enters and sees a dead place, "air brown as an old daguerreotype fading." First, furniture recalls for him the place of his family and childhood; the bed, the place of conception. The time of conception is not a time to be known, and thus the poet refuses to look at the date on the old newspapers spread over the bed. "The old Morris chair bought soon / After marriage," that's next. Some representation of the father is there with remembered features, "the big head" and "the big nose." At first he does not look at the eyes, but when he does, they are not there, because the poet sees only a skeletal past. Only the sensuous impressions of the father, now long dead, are there for the poet to know. And the father says nothing, though he had spoken cryptically and dramatically in all other poems of the past. The "eyes / Had been blue," but they "stare out at / Nothing." The times and the father of old have said all they can ever say to the present.

The mother's eyes had been brown, and she too sits in "the accustomed rocker" without motion. Even her dress has rotted. She too is a skeleton, and even her lap is "shrouded femurs." Now there are no "Lips to kiss with," and only the things which are where the eyes once had been now stare. And they have "no fire on the cold hearth now, / To stare at." The Christmas tree is "denuded," although there are still three packages, one for each of the children. The memory plays tricks, and the poet steps to find out which package is his, but he hears an italicized and remembered voice from the past: *"No presents, son, till the little ones come."*

Three empty chairs sit in the room—one for each of the children, the largest chair for the poet, one for the sister, and a "little red chair" for the youngest. The past is empty, like the chairs, empty of all but the poet in his dreams: *"They're empty, they're empty, but me—oh, I'm here!"* The elegiac grief has become so broad and great that it extends not only to the dead mother and father but also to the living who are no longer there. The world of that family has vanished as surely as death. What the poet is revealing here is a world of the beloved past from which all—people, time, and place—have vanished except for the one who grieves for all that is gone. "Suddenly, / Silence /- And no / Breath comes."

Two parts of the poem turn to Warren's immediate time and place, the city: "blunt crowd," fumes and smog, a woman in an asylum for the insane, clerks going home, and the citizens of the coming night. Then after a memory of a visit to the Nez Percé Pass and its snows, he asks

> But tell me, tell me,
> Will I never know
> What present there was in that package for me,
> Under the Christmas tree?

The intensity of the speaker suggests that the gift may be the ultimate truth. Warren has recently commented that the package contains "his whole life, of course."[95]

The poem ends stating that in the world of his dream "all things are continuous": the past and the present; reality and dream; logic and the natural and fantasy and the supernatural —whatever opposites about this poetic family that exist dreamt and undreamt.

> This
> Is the process whereby pain of the past in its pastness
> May be converted into the future tense
>
> Of joy.

The future tense is a ponderable. Most simply, it is the remaining life of Warren and the recollections of the dead that will linger with him. One cannot be certain, however, that there is not more. For one who describes his theological beliefs as those only of a yearner, Warren uses words (like "future tense / Of joy") which open vistas of unknown and undeterminable and perhaps infinite worlds.

In the last volume, *Being Here,* Warren returns to the geography of Todd County, to his first explorations of that world, and finally to his early profound puzzlements over the world and himself in that environment. Todd County and Guthrie are close to the famous cave country of Kentucky, and the earth is undercut by hundreds of underground streams and "sink holes." Near Cave City, not far away, Warren writes, is the site of the cave in which the unfortunate Floyd Collins in the most spectacular newsstory of the world before that date lost his life early in the century during Warren's younger days. Warren or the persona found a cave when he was six: "Each summer I came, in twilight peered in, crept further, / Till one summer all I could see was a gray / Blotch of light far behind."

Then at twelve, he came with a flashlight, and crawled in the cave far back enough to see stalactites and to find "far down, far down" an underground stream. He cuts off his light and meditates on himself and being: *"This is me.* Thought: *Me— who am I?"* Years later he thinks the same thoughts: *"This is me.* / And thought: *Who am I?* . . . / And in darkness . . . even asked: *Is this all? What is all?"*

The cave is real, Warren has said, but obviously it is also philosophical, Platonic, even religious. Typically, the poem ends with a question. Perhaps when the poet is seventy-five it is a poem of more than yearning. The poet does not assert merely disbelief. He asks of identity and existence and life whether this is all and, whether or not it is, *"What is all?"* And with this poem in *Being Here,* that is where the yearning and the question rest—for the moment.

The entire poem "October Picnic Long Ago" is printed separately as a sort of prologue to *Being Here* and perhaps for all the volumes. Warren indicates his recognition of the beginnings of his life and of the origins of his best poetry. It is printed in italics —set off by type as well as by position. In quality and subject matter, the poem is worthy of its unique position.

"October Picnic" is a dream, an idyll, a memory of a picnic
—late in the year, perhaps as the poem is late in Warren's life
—but at a perfect time. *"And over us all, in a flood, poured the
golden October light."*

The family is both intimate and formal. After the liveryman,
Bumbo, hands the reins to the *"mister"* (or father), the mother
and three children, identical to Robert and Mary and Thomas
Warren, get settled and fixed in the vehicle. Then they journey
out of the world. *"Out of town, clop-clop, till we found a side-lane
that led / Into woods, where gold leaves flicked a fairy shadow and
light."*

The picnic and the setting are as formal and perfect as a
Japanese garden. It is set off from all the ictuses of horror and
violence in *Brother to Dragons* and the tragic poems such as those
about the Gillums and Dr. Knox. It is a peaceful island of the
mind. *"A grass circle, and off to one side a boulder, a spring, / All
ready for us, and a crude fireplace of stone."* This is the place and
the time of an Eden in one's life. Perfect and formal and natural,
it is the time *"before the auto had come."* Even the mother's skirt
is blue serge, and *"My father's suede shoes were buttoned up high,
and a Norfolk jacket."* The people and the scene come out of the
past, but the poem stands outside of all time. The perfections
are not of Warren's world. In one sense, they are not of the
world of realities and violence that Warren has always created;
in another sense they are of some dream world, some past time
that floats off into something beyond death, into eternity. The
parents, *"hand in hand,"* are engaged *"in one long conversation /
That even now I can't think has had an end— / But where?"*

A good part of the island picnic is an impossible illusion.
"Picnics have ends." In deliberately stilted speech, the mother
exclaims, *"Could a place so beautiful be!"* Then, even in the idyll,
there is the old note of the failure of the father amid his joys:
"My ship will come in yet."

So the dream family returns, at least for the time, to the
world. The mother is joyful: *"she gaily sang / . . . as she sang."*
But going homeward she sings among sly shadows that
"Leashed the Future up, like a hound with a slavering fang." As yet
the seven-year-old boy does not know what a Future is, but

there is one, and it is there, even if it is not to be thought about on this perfect day. But there is still the future with the slavering fang, and even after the knowledge of the fang, the poem ends with a one-line stanza of joy: *"And she sang."* The poem is beautiful for Warren; it is an island away from reality and violence and original sin and the pain. It is a relief from the struggles and the hells of this world. Perhaps the poem in the context of the total works of its creator is more beautiful because of the known realities of all the ugliness that can be a part of Warren's philosophies and the worlds he has known, or created. More than any other work he has written, this poem indicates that sometimes there can be another world to flee to.

Often in the latest volume, *Being Here,* the poet's mind returns to extraordinarily intimate and lyrical memories of the lives of his family. He remembers waking one night when "all the house [was] at rest" and wondering why he, a boy, woke. He hears the snores of mother and father and "loudest of all that of my old grandfather / Who with years now struggled, grumbling, croupy, and slow, / But one night had roused to a blood-yell, dreaming Fort Pillow or Shiloh." For no definable reason the boy wanders outside and sees "the tracks of my bare / Dark footprints set in the moonlit dew like snow, / And thought: *I go where they go, for they must know where we go."* The contemplation or the figure, whatever it is, is complex as it is imaginative and brilliant. The tracks *do* know where we have been, and where it has been determined that we will go. The past creates the future. This seems not to be a suggestion of determinism, but poetic recollection or realization that our dispositions—our selves—which made us go where we have been help us to know where we will walk in the dark and dew-covered grass of the future.

The tracks follow the remembered child "down to a stream" where the cattle stare "through the dream that I was." Dream and reality become inseparable. The "realness I was, it must lie asleep yonder / In the far, white house that was part of the moonlight's dream, too. / Then blankness." At the coming of day the boy rushes home where "all seemed still, as still as the dead."

And they are dead. Except in the mind of the poet. Reality insists to the much older poet that they are not dead in his memory and in the poem. "Not dead! Though long years now are, and the creek bulldozed dry." Time at the end of the poem is complex. Even in the present tense, the poet says that "At sixty per I am whirled past the spot where my blood / Is unwitting." That is, in part, his kin do not know. But here even the present tense (*am whirled*) is memory and is also the past, some time before the composition of the poem. Later after the whirling by, he does remember, and he relives the past, and he writes the poem with awareness and consciousness that he had never known before.

These poems, finally, and fragments of other poems that form a piece with the longer works, form an autobiography, biographies, and histories in verse. They are personal, regional, and historical in dimensions and scope. As poetry they cover a territory much larger than the number of pages it takes to print them. The time span—from just after the Civil War perhaps until the moment when Warren's pen is stilled—is less extensive than the saga of Faulkner. But, as poetry, they are more compact, even than Faulkner. At first glance, Warren seems to explicate his own writing, even to moralize, but lasting contemplation produces statements, concrete and abstract, general and specific, as puzzling as the contents of that unopened box under the Christmas tree. The connections between Warren's poems have never been explicitly stated in his volumes of poetry; they may only be deduced by a reader or a critic. Nevertheless they assume a unity from the singularity of the life of the poet, from a consistent tone and subject matter, from progressions of chronology in the lives of a family and a nation, and from the meaning of an endless and insatiable thirst for knowledge and search for truth. To treat the poems as something of a unit, as here, is unquestionably a momentary violation of the unity of each distinct work of art and, perhaps, sometimes of the whole body of Warren's work. They are like, say, an experimental and looseleaf French novel. However the pages are shuffled and ordered, they come out with oneness as well as separateness. The intentional fallacy may work (or fail) from two perspectives. If one cannot measure a work by the author's intent, he also cannot deny the truth though it was not conscious or intended. Thus literature is pervaded by the unintentional truth as much as criticism is by the intentional fallacy. That truth in the separate poems about Warren's family, his friend, and his self is a unity of spiritual search.

Robert Penn Warren is a major poet by any standard—perhaps even a prophet in some meanings of the word. He has had a sustained career as a poet for some sixty years. At an age when most are living and lecturing on the basis of their past creations, Warren continues to write profoundly, precisely, and beautifully. Since the *Selected Poems: 1973–1975* (published in 1976), he has published *Now and Then* (1978), *Being Here* (1980), and *Rumor Verified* (1981). Another volume is scheduled for 1982 and he has completed a longer poem on Chief Joseph. *Brother to Dragons* may be the best long unified single poem yet written in America. "Mortmain," "The Ballad of Billie Potts," and *Audubon* are significant and substantial. Warren is probably the most accomplished American narrative poet.

In the family and community poems considered in this volume, Warren has created a complex and extensive world. No American author seems to have started out with a design for the creation of his own literary community in several works, but many there are who have persistently developed works about their cultures and their places. Warren's people—even in this imaginary Kentucky community without a name—derive from and represent a world as recognizably Warren's as Yoknapatawpha is Faulkner's or Winesburg, Ohio, is Anderson's. The community exists in Warren's poetic works, although neither poet nor critic can pinpoint the time when he came to recognize its existence.

The poetic chronicle of Warren's family has a scope of more than a hundred years, not less than the time span of the Gant (or Webber) and Sartoris and Compson families or of the political and literary sagas of the Lowells and the Adamses. The joys and sorrows of the Penns and the Warrens are created with lyrical intensity and with national and historical implications.

What Faulkner was perhaps groping for when he wrote *Flags in the Dust* is reflected in a different form in Warren's poems of the personal and community past.

The community past and the family past give the poems a texture different from that usually found in the fiction. The poems about the past reveal that the deep feelings almost always concealed beneath the hard exteriors of the narrators in Warren's best novels are indeed related to the personal and lyrical feelings of the poet.

In the diverse poems, the dominant theme seems to be the desire to know. The effectiveness of this motif is due in part to its final failure. There are moments of joy and even of reconcilement, but one cannot achieve ultimate joy in the labor of the frontier, the relationships of the family, the completeness of knowledge, and the beauties of art, or in the knowledge of the amazing grace of personal or religious salvation.

References

WRITINGS BY ROBERT PENN WARREN

1. "A Conversation with Cleanth Brooks," in *The Possibilities of Order: Cleanth Brooks and His Work,* ed. Lewis P. Simpson (Baton Rouge: Louisiana State University Press, 1976), pp. 28-29.
2. "Elizabeth Madox Roberts: Life Is from Within," *Saturday Review* 46 (March 2, 1963), 20.
3. In *Fugitives' Reunion,* ed. Rob Roy Purdy (Nashville: Vanderbilt University Press, 1959), p. 142.
4. p. 151.
5. *Jefferson Davis Gets His Citizenship Back* (Lexington: The University Press of Kentucky, 1980), pp. 4-7.
6. p. 10.
7. p. 15.
8. "Mightier Than the Sword," *Yale Political* 1 (February 1962), 17.
9. In *Poet's Choice,* ed. Paul Engle and Joseph Langland (New York: Dial Press, 1962), p. 80.
10. *Selected Essays* (New York: Random House, 1958), p. 26.
11. p. 33.
12. p. 268.
13. p. 270.
14. *Selected Poems of Herman Melville: A Reader's Edition* (New York: Random House, 1970), p. 11.
15. *John Greenleaf Whittier's Poetry: An Appraisal and a Selection* (Minneapolis: University of Minnesota Press), 1971, p. 34.

BY ROBERT PENN WARREN WITH OTHERS

16. Cleanth Brooks, R. W. B. Lewis, and Robert Penn Warren, *American Literature: The Makers and the Making,* 2 vols. paged continuously (New York: St. Martin's, 1973), p. xiii.
17. pp. 549-50.
18. p. 1626.
19. p. 2257.

20. Cleanth Brooks and Robert Penn Warren, *Understanding Poetry: An Anthology for College Students* (New York: Henry Holt), 1938 edition, p. iv.
21. 1950 edition, p. xxi.
22. 1960 edition, p. xiv.

PUBLISHED INTERVIEWS

23. Joseph Rosenbloom, "Robert Penn Warren at 72," *Boston Globe,* 17 April 1977, p. 27.
24. Robert Penn Warren , "A Conversation with Cleanth Brooks," in *The Possibilities of Order: Cleanth Brooks and His Work,* ed. Lewis P. Simpson (Baton Rouge: Louisiana State University Press, 1976), pp. 28-29.
25. Floyd C. Watkins, "A Dialogue with Robert Penn Warren on *Brother to Dragons," The Southern Review* 16 (Winter 1980), 11.

Interviews in *Robert Penn Warren Talking: Interviews 1950-1978,* ed. Floyd C. Watkins and John T. Hiers (New York: Random House, 1980):

26. "Robert Penn Warren (A Self-Interview)," pp. 3-5.
27. Ralph Ellison and Eugene Walter, "Warren on the Art of Fiction," p. 28.
28. "An Interview with Flannery O'Connor and Robert Penn Warren," p. 69.
29. C. Vann Woodward, "The Uses of History in Fiction," pp. 93, 95.
30. Richard B. Sale, "An Interview in New Haven with Robert Penn Warren," p. 102.
31. pp. 106-7.
32. p. 115.
33. p. 121.
34. Ruth Fisher, "A Conversation with Robert Penn Warren," pp. 139-40.
35. Edwin Newman, "Speaking Freely," p. 163.
36. portion of the above interview not published; transcript is in Watkins Papers (see 95).
37. Marshall Walker, "Robert Penn Warren: An Interview," p. 175.
38. pp. 189-90.
39. Peter Stitt, "An Interview with Robert Penn Warren," p. 224.
40. p. 229.

41. p. 232.
42. pp. 236-37.
43. John Baker, "A Conversation with Robert Penn Warren," pp. 238-42.
44. p. 254.
45. "Interview with Eleanor Clark and Robert Penn Warren," p. 263.
46. *New England Review* 1 (Autumn 1978), 56 (original publication of above interview, which is not complete in *Warren Talking*).
47. "Dick Cavett: An Interview with Robert Penn Warren," p. 281.
48. portion of the above interview not published; transcript in Watkins Papers (see 95).

UNPUBLISHED INTERVIEWS

49. Interview by David Farrell with Robert Penn Warren, October 6, 1977, in the Robert Penn Warren Oral History Project (Department of Special Collections and Archives, University of Kentucky Library), p. 3.
50. p. 7.
51. p. 10.
52. pp. 15-16.
53. pp. 19-22.
54. pp. 25-27.
55. p. 55.

Interviews conducted by Will Fridy, records of which are in the Oral History Office, Department of History, Western Kentucky University:

56. George Street Boone, February 4, 1977.
57. Joy Bale Boone, April 7, 1977.
58. Sara Carneal, February 17, 1978.
59. Mrs. Hugh B. Disharoon, February 4, 1977.
60. Matthew Finn, February 10, 1977.
61. N. Everett Frey, February 10, 1977.
62. Kent Greenfield, February 3, 1977.
63. Lester Lannom, February 3, 1977.
64. Frances Marion Williams, February 4, 1977.

Interviews conducted by Floyd C. Watkins, records of which are in the Floyd C. Watkins Papers, Woodruff Library, Emory University:

65. Thomas M. Allensworth, Sr., summer, 1976.
66. Richard Bourne, Nashville, Tennessee, summer, 1976.

67. Cleanth Brooks, New Haven, Connecticut, summer, 1977.
68. Eloise Hamill Carney, Nashville, Tennessee, summer, 1976.
69. John R. Claypool, Nashville, Tennessee, 1976.
70. Everett Frey, Guthrie, Kentucky, summer, 1976.
71. Paul Gardner, Cerulean, Kentucky, summer, 1977.
72. Kent Greenfield, summer, 1977.
73. Evelyn Hooser, summer, 1977.
74. Lester Lannom (by telephone), summer, 1976.
75. Dorothy McElwain, summer, 1976.
76. W. C. McGhee, Nolensville, Tennessee, summer, 1977.
77. Hermit Mitchell, Cerulean, Kentucky, summer, 1977.
78. Sara Frances Rascoe, Cerulean, Kentucky, summer, 1977.
79. Charlene Ring, Franklin, Tennessee, summer, 1977.
80. Allen Tate, Nashville, Tennessee, summer, 1976.
81. Robert Penn Warren, January, 1979.
82. Thomas Warren, summer, 1976.
83. Thomas Warren, summer, 1977.
84. Frances Marion Williams, summer, 1977.

MANUSCRIPT SOURCES

Allen Tate Papers, Princeton University Library:

88. Warren to Tate, early spring, 1924.
89. Warren to Tate, July 11, 1925.
90. Warren to Tate, February 6, 1926.
91. Warren to Tate, 1927.
92. Warren to Tate, January 15, 1966.

Donald Davidson Collection, Joint University Libraries, Nashville, Tennessee:

85. Warren to Davidson, 1927.
86. Warren to Davidson, June 23, 1928.

Katherine Ann Porter Papers, Yale University Library:

87. Porter to Warren, February 4, 1955.

Robert Penn Warren Papers, University of Kentucky Library:

93. Carbon copy of manuscript of speech by Warren on March 26, 1962, at Robert Frost's birthday party in Washington, D.C.
94. Manuscript poem.

Floyd C. Watkins Papers, Woodruff Library, Emory University:

95. Letters, Warren to Watkins; manuscripts annotated by Warren; tapes and transcripts of interviews. Access to this collection is restricted.

SOURCES FOR LOCAL AND FAMILY HISTORY

Note: Except where otherwise indicated I have taken dates and genealogical information from the cemetery where the Warrens are buried in Cerulean, from census reports, or from Eurie Pearl Wilford Neel, *The Statistical Handbook of Trigg County Kentucky The Gateway to the Jackson Purchase in Kentucky and Tennessee,* 3 (Nashville: Rich Printing Company, 1961).

96. J. H. Battle and W. H. Perrin, *Counties of Todd and Christian, Kentucky: Historical and Biographical* (Chicago and Louisville: F. A. Battey Publishing Co., 1884), p. 181.
97. p. 193.
98. William Edward Fitch, *Mineral Waters of the United States and American Spas* (Philadelphia and New York: Lea & Febiger, 1927).
99. Thomas W. Herringshaw, ed. and comp, *Local and National Poets with Interesting Biographical Sketches and Choice Selections from Over One Thousand Living American Poets* (Chicago: American Publishers' Association, 1890), p. 88.
100. John Berrien Lindsley, *The Military Annals of Tennessee: Confederate,* First Series (Nashville: J. M. Lindsley & Co., 1886), pp. 724-32. Contains a regimental history of the Fifteenth Tennessee Cavalry. Captain G. T. Penn is listed as commander of Company H, but the activities of that company in the numerous battles of the regiment are not mentioned.
101. Virginia G. and Lewis G. Pedigo, *History of Patrick and Henry Counties Virginia* (Baltimore: Regional Publishing Company, 1977), pp. 220-23.
102. Trigg County, Kentucky, Deed Book Q 235.
103. Deed Book X 272.
104. *The War of the Rebellion: A Compilation of the Official Records of Union and Confederate Armies,* 70 vols. (Washington, D.C., 1880-1901), series 1, vol. 32, part 3, p. 609.

OTHER REFERENCES

105. Charles H. Bohner, *Robert Penn Warren* (New York: Twayne, 1964), p. 21.
106. Cleanth Brooks, *American Literature: A Mirror, Lens or Prism?*, Sir George Watson Lecture delivered in the University of Leicester 28 April 1966 (Leicester University Press, 1967).
107. F. Garvin Davenport, Jr., *The Myth of Southern History* (Nashville: Vanderbilt University Press, 1970), p. 139.
108. Donald Davidson, *Southern Writers in the Modern World*, Eugenia Dorothy Blount Memorial Lectures, 1957 (Athens: University of Georgia Press, 1958), pp. 40-41.
109. Joe Davis, "Robert Penn Warren and the Journey to the West," *Modern Fiction Studies* 6 (Spring 1960), 73-82.
110. William F. Dwyer, "Light Religiously Dim: The Poetry of Robert Penn Warren," *Fresco* 1 (1960), 52.
111. F. Cudworth Flint, "Robert Penn Warren," *American Oxonian* 34 (April 1947), 76.
112. James Hastings, ed., *Encyclopaedia of Religion and Ethics* (New York: Scribner's, 1910), 2:779-80, 782.
113. M. L. Rosenthal, "Robert Penn Warren's Poetry," *South Atlantic Quarterly* 62 (Autumn 1963), 500-501.
114. Louis D. Rubin, *The Wary Fugitives: Four Poets and the South* (Baton Rouge: Louisiana State University Press, 1978), pp. 332-33.
115. William Tjenos, "The Poetry of Robert Penn Warren: The Art to Transfigure," *Southern Literary Journal* 9 (1976), 3, 4.
116. James Wright, "The Stiff Smile of Mr. Warren," *Kenyon Review* 20 (Autumn 1958), 647.

Index